BBQ
ALLSTARS

46 00
5200
68,80
68,80
64,80
64,80

FANNING THE FLAMES

OTHER BOOKS BY MELISSA COOKSTON

Smokin' in the Boys' Room

Smokin' Hot in the South

FANNING THE FLAMES

RECIPES AND TALL TALES FROM BBQ HALL OF FAMER MELISSA COOKSTON

Foreword by Michael Symon
Photography by Ken Goodman

Achiote Rotisserie Chicken (page 112)

CONTENTS

HANKS
Yazoo's Q
DELTA

FOREWORD

The first time I met Melissa Cookston was at the Memphis in May International Festival in 2010. Mike Mills, "The Legend," was walking me through the grounds introducing me to the heavy hitters of barbecue. When he introduced me to Melissa, he leaned over and said, "Bet on her to win Whole Hog." She did. Then she won Grand Champion, too.

Melissa wasn't only the first woman to win the Whole Hog category. She was also the first female pitmaster to win Grand Champion . . . TWICE!

In a field dominated by men, she didn't just compete; she set the standard. She wasn't trying to prove herself. She was doing what she always does: cooking extraordinary barbecue with the precision and confidence that only come from hard work and obsession with the craft.

What I respect most about her philosophy is her openness. Melissa doesn't believe barbecue belongs to a chosen few. She believes it belongs to anyone willing to learn. She shares everything she knows so others can find their own fire. That mindset has made her more than a champion. It's made her a teacher, a restaurateur, and an author.

The title "winningest woman in barbecue" is earned. When she became the first woman inducted into the Barbecue Hall of Fame, it was overdue recognition for someone who changed the trajectory of the sport. But her real legacy is what she gives back through teaching, mentoring, and inspiring the next generation of pitmasters.

Her newest book, *Fanning the Flames,* continues that mission. If her first book made barbecue approachable, this one elevates it. It's a reflection of her evolution through travel, experience, and years of tending the fire. The recipes come from a lifetime of lessons, each one grounded in authenticity and flavor.

Melissa never forgets where she came from—the cold mornings by the pit, the long nights learning what worked. She learned barbecue the hard way, so when she teaches, it's with heart and conviction.

If you're new to barbecue or have spent a lifetime at the smoker, Melissa will meet you where you are. She'll teach you, challenge you, and inspire you to fan your own flames.

—Michael Symon

INTRODUCTION

A lot has changed in the world of BBQ since I wrote my first cookbook, *Smokin' in the Boys' Room*. I wrote that book as my "origin story," in which I told recipes and stories about my upbringing, why I cook the way I do, and what my belief in Memphis-style BBQ entails. The book's main premise that I wanted to express was "ease of entry." So many people make BBQ and grilling out to be some mystical experience with the secrets known only to a select few. They're not. They're a great way to add flavor to your meal and spice to your life. But there is no real BBQ Yoda somewhere waiting to impart the secrets of life to you through an amazing pulled pork recipe.

Since I wrote that book, I've traveled a lot, cooked even more, and met some fantastic people. I've cooked all across the United States, hosted a James Beard dinner, and been to (and cooked in) places from Abu Dhabi to Cusco, Peru. I've won some more awards, retired from competition BBQ, started a foundation to teach young adults to cook, and caused a lot of mischief. And I feel like I'm just getting started.

My BBQ Journey

BBQ has been good to me. I mean, really good. I've been on TV shows, opened restaurants, written cookbooks, and met some wonderful people because of BBQ. I've been able to travel across the country and internationally, meeting people and tasting great food. I've learned about cooking on an intrinsic, fundamental level. I've learned about the absolute wealth of flavors available to use. I've been exposed to some of the best food I have ever tasted, thanks to my BBQ roots.

I was born in Ruleville, a small town in the Mississippi Delta. Ruleville is a little spot on the road a few miles east of Cleveland. Cleveland is a few miles south of Clarksdale, home of the "crossroads" where Robert Johnson sold his soul to the devil. (I wasn't there to witness the transaction, but old-timers in the area swear it happened.) Indianola, where B. B. King grew up, is just a few miles away. My parents ended up in Greenville, also in the Mississippi Delta region. We lived there until I was around ten years old; then my mother, younger brother, and I moved to Pontotoc, on the northeastern side of the state. Pontotoc is a few miles west of Tupelo, the birthplace of Elvis. Music is a big thing in Mississippi. Also a big thing: barbecue.

My first memory of enjoying BBQ was when my grandfather Quinton would take me to his local coffee shop, which was also the only BBQ joint in town. The smell of pork cooking in a pit was intoxicating. Sometimes, if there was enough farming advice, tall tales about the size of a caught fish, or just socializing, we would stay long enough to get a BBQ sandwich. That was the best BBQ of my childhood. I'm not sure if it was really the BBQ that I liked or the company I was keeping.

Restaurants and food have always played a big role in my life. I started working in restaurants when I was thirteen years old. I somehow cajoled my (underage) way into a job at the local drive-in, where I worked as a fountain girl. (If you want a slushy, I can make it.) From my not-so-epic career start, I continued to work in local restaurants as either a primary or secondary job. I had started doing paralegal work, but office work and I just disagreed. Restaurants somehow get into your blood—the chaos, the smells, the incredible feeling when a shift runs well, the struggles when you have demanding guests.

I didn't do more than dabble in the "back of house" operations until I started working for corporate restaurants. But when I was finally allowed in the kitchen, I knew I had found my happy place.

I started cooking in barbecue contests in 1996. The main "circuit" of contests in my area were the (then) Memphis in May–sanctioned BBQ contests. Memphis in May (as we refer to the more-than-a-mouthful Memphis in May World Championship Barbecue Cooking Contest) has always been the holy grail for BBQ aficionados in the Mid-South. On one of our first dates, my now-husband took me to a BBQ contest. Smelling the air, redolent with hickory smoke, spice, and pork; seeing the teams sweeping the ground in preparation for judges; watching the pitmasters (of course, no one called them that back then—that's a TV word) spin tall tales of the origins of their pig and why the judges were about to taste nirvana on a rib bone . . . I knew I was hooked the minute I got there. It appealed to my competitive nature and love of BBQ.

Within a few months, we were ready to compete. I drafted my brother to help, and we put together a ragtag compilation of tents, smokers, tables, and other supplies and entered a contest in Greenwood, Mississippi. On the way down, most of our tent poles fell off the trailer, so we spent a good part of the day looking for substitutes. We entered pork shoulders in the contest, which occurred during an unseasonal rain-bringing cold front. I spent the night huddled under the hot box of my smoker, "Betsy," trying to stay dry and keep the smoker running. It was a miserable weekend, and I swore my nascent career as a BBQ competitor would be over as soon as I could get back home. Then I got a trophy for fifth place in Shoulders, and that silly trophy set me on the path I've followed ever since.

My husband, Pete, and I both had restaurant jobs, and BBQ contests are time-intensive and expensive. Over the next several years, we entered when we could and did well for very part-timers. My ribs consistently won awards, but whole hog was my true love. Getting better at it was a slow, long climb, but every time I cooked one, I tried to learn something new. The worst job at a BBQ contest is cleaning up a whole hog after judging, especially when you lose. Sticking your head in a hot smoker on a hot July day in the South to pick the meat from the hog and clean the cooker is draining. But every time I cooked, I would stand there afterward and pull the remaining meat from the hog, looking at every piece. I would check the moisture, the texture, and how the flavor had permeated it. I learned a lot. I adjusted times and temperatures. I looked at how I was flavoring the meat and adjusted it. I also learned to pull meat for judges and which pieces were the best. The way I cook hogs today is very similar to the way I cooked them way back when. I've made some simple adjustments with big results, but the process is the same. Not winning when

I started wasn't about my messing up hogs. (Well, most of the time it wasn't.) It was more about my learning to properly showcase the best parts to judges and ensure each bite was flavorful, moist, and tender.

In 2007 we decided to throw caution to the wind and enter contests full time. It was a tough decision and had harsh consequences. We lived a feast-or-famine life. Go to a contest and lose, it would be tuna salad sandwiches for a while. (To this day, I still hate tuna salad sandwiches.) However, something magical happens when you cook BBQ every single day and enter contests every single week: You start to get consistent. You learn to look at every piece of raw meat and know how you should cook it to allow its best attributes to shine. You quit worrying about the weather as you just naturally adjust your methods. Timing your cooking to ensure it is perfect right at judging time becomes second nature. You learn how to manage a clean-burning fire. You start to actually get good at cooking BBQ, no matter the circumstance.

In 2008 I finally entered the Memphis in May contest, and we made the finals in the hog division. In the "Memphis-style" BBQ contest, the categories are pork shoulders, pork ribs (almost everyone cooks baby back ribs), and whole hogs. The top three highest-scoring entries in each category in the preliminary judging round go to a second round of judging—the finals. Four judges visit each of the nine teams in the finals and rate them top to bottom. We were in pop-up tents and on a dirt floor, competing against teams that spent thousands of dollars on their booth alone. We came in third and learned a lot. I managed a respectable

sixth place the following year with a hog I thought deserved much better. In 2010 we got lucky and won the whole hog and Grand Champion. It was a fantastic day. I've won five more world championships since then, and it's a legacy I'm very proud to have made.

In 2017 I received a phone call from the Barbecue Hall of Fame informing me that I was being inducted. I was driving at the time and had to pull over to turn around and look in the back seat to see if there were cameras recording because I was being pranked. I didn't think I was deserving at that point in my career, but I was thrilled and humbled to be included.

Since then I have been fortunate to have many more amazing days, both in the competition world and in travels, meeting great chefs and learning new things. Every day is a gift, and I want to know more!

This Book

I have always been a Delta girl. The Delta region of the Mississippi River is deemed to start (at least culturally) around Memphis and end in New Orleans. Unfortunately, a lot of that culture has revolved around poverty, inequity, and struggle. However, out of that struggle usually spring some beautiful flowers: blues music with real soul, colorful folk art, and an ability to turn poor ingredients into amazing food.

Mississippi is a unique place in the world and has shaped everything about me. Trust me, there are plenty of reasons to take issue with Mississippi but a lot more to be thankful about. One thing that we're only slowly absorbing, however, is new flavors. We've always been insulated, and most folks in Mississippi are okay with that. Our cuisine has been influenced by our neighbors, by the bounty of the land, and by the poverty of our beginnings. We make do. We don't look for help, though we're thankful when it's offered. There is nothing wrong with serving food in its simple, fresh, and flavorful goodness.

However, I like to taste the world. I want to see the same culture in other people's food, just as I can see and taste Mississippi through ours. Moreover, I generally want to taste food cooked over an open flame.

I've always been one step away from a pyromaniac. No, not the type who commits arson (although my husband once took a flamethrower away from me) but the kind who loves cooking with fire. My love of cooking BBQ morphed into all things grilled. Flames are mesmerizing and wild, allowing you to conquer the untamed, even for just a quick meal. We love grilled foods for their intrinsically better flavors. We love cooking with flames because it's fun. If you look at any culture, there is a tradition of flame cooking and grilling.

Smoke and Fire

It is essential to understand a couple of things while looking at the recipes in this book. First, I am not a "truist." That means I don't believe BBQ must be done one way. I do follow the path of smoke and fire, but if cooking a pork butt in the slow cooker with some BBQ sauce makes you happy, then I'm all for it. If you enjoy the challenge of a smoker or want to taste the beautiful sear on a steak over a hot flame, I'm your girl. But you can make something that tastes *almost* as good in your kitchen, and I'm okay with that, too.

Secondly, I believe BBQ is the first true sous vide food, and exploring the different time-temperature relationships with whatever you are cooking is vital in exploring barbecue and food in general. I know that *sous vide* means "under vacuum." I am also aware that you can cook a beef short rib sous vide for seventy-two hours and it comes out succulent, tender, and with a medium-rare appearance; or you can braise it for four hours in the oven and achieve the same texture and flavor (though not the appearance). Some argue over taste, some over methods, and others over ingredients. I'm all for the arguments. I'm just here to present the different ways of cooking. Let the fighting begin.

For example, let's talk about low and slow. I'm a Memphis-style barbecuer. That means pork shoulders or butts are pulled only by hand, separating any fats from the juicy, delectable pork. (A pox on any restaurant that chops pork. It is an excuse to cut corners, but I digress.) So to achieve pullable pork, you need to follow a few rules: For a typical pork butt (eight to ten pounds) at 225°F, you'll need to cook it for twelve to fourteen hours, and the internal temperature of the butt may register 180°F. At 250°F, you'll need to cook the butt for eight to ten hours, and the internal may come up to 195°F. At 275°F, you'll need to cook it for seven hours and let it rest for an hour, and the internal temperature may be 202°F to 205°F. Like sous vide cooking, BBQ's time-temperature relationship is real and should be followed.

In these examples, all the textures of the finished pulled pork will be similar but not the same. The hotter and faster you cook (and the shorter the cooking time), the denser the end product will feel in your mouth. Now, since you aren't sampling pork from each temperature at one sitting, you won't notice the difference, but I want you to know how the relationship works.

In the past, BBQ competitors generally cooked at temperatures of 225°F to 250°F. In the past few years, they have increased the temps to 275°F to 325°F. Resting time is very important when you cook at these temperatures as it allows the collagens and fats to melt into the meats. Normally, in a low and slow cook, this would happen within the cooking process. Sometimes, especially in large pieces of meat such as a whole hog, you will see the internal temperature decline even as you reach finishing temperatures.

In the recipes in this book, I will present time frames for the grill or ask you to set up a "two-zone fire." Don't fret if you can't follow everything exactly; BBQ is not an exact science. When I teach a class, I first tell people to expect the unexpected. The people who know only how to follow a recipe are the first to get bowled over in a contest. (I used to pray for bad weather at a contest; I've cooked and won competitions in thunderstorms, hail, crazy winds, and even remnants of hurricanes.) Adapt to the occasion and keep on cooking!

ADAPTING RECIPES

When you don't have much money, you'd better learn how to season food.

Mississippi is the definition of "peasant cooking." We have a long tradition of having to "make do" and still serve beautiful, wonderfully seasoned meals.

In this book, I'll discuss cooking, travels, celebrations, and favorite recipes. I want this to be a grilling, smoking, cooking, and good food resource for you. (And for me; as I age, I find myself looking up my own recipes more and more!) I'll also discuss grilling-centric meals. But why pigeonhole us? Let's talk about good food.

I have always cooked with a little bit of a what-if in my head. What if I did this? What if I did that? Sometimes the results are spectacular, and other times the results end with my trying to hide that I was cooking before going out to dinner. We have a saying at our house: "There's always pizza." While changing recipes is something I do often to see what the results of a modification would be, it is paramount to understand that no recipe is 100 percent replicable. Let me repeat: No recipe can be repeated exactly—ever.

What's the point of cookbooks, blogs, and recipes in general, then? They are guides that help us create something in our kitchens, whether simple meals or extravagant undertakings. They are sparks meant to inspire you to create and enjoy food, and what could be better than that? Most of all, a good recipe is a guide that shows you how something should be cooked in an ideal environment, but it also gives you tips on what to do when life gives you a few more lemons than you wanted.

When I say no recipe is replicable, understand that most recipes will get you very close to the expected result. However, it will not be exactly as it was when the chef created the recipe. When dealing with food items, we must understand that they are all different. A pear this week may be of the same variety, but it is slightly riper than one you tried two days ago. A pork butt may have more (or less) marbling or may be trimmed differently during processing and may cook slightly differently. At my restaurant, we go through tons of ribs every week, and we are very tight in our specs for them. However, one rib may have beautiful intrinsic marbling and the next may have more extraneous fat pockets. It happens—different times of the year for harvesting, different finishing feeds, slightly different genetics, the amount of rain, or the soil in which something was grown all have an impact. Added together, many minor variances can have a major impact on the results of a recipe.

Just as necessary to discuss, or perhaps even more so, are the differences in your cooking equipment. We all know that a cheaper skillet may not heat evenly, and varying brands of ovens may cook slightly differently. We learn to use the tools we have. Without testing and experience, we may not know how long to heat our skillets, or what rack to place the lasagna on, but we can adapt. Different models and brands of grills have even more variance, plus the added complication of cooking in differing conditions. Wind, ambient temperature, or precipitation will change your cooking results on any grill. When we are trying to write recipes for multiple grills, the possible outcomes are tough to predict.

That's why I say you won't be able to replicate these recipes exactly. I will throw in some advice, but I can't address every situation. The best thing you can do as an aspiring cook/chef/pitmaster/grilling guru is to learn to adapt. If there is one thing I hope you take away from this cookbook, it is that the ability to adapt is a true cook's (especially a true barbecuer's) best friend.

When I started cooking on the BBQ circuit, the equipment we used was, relative to today, "sketchy." I started cooking on a huge offset barrel grill named Betsy. It was a challenge in the best of weather and a downright Herculean task in inclement conditions. To maintain the grill's moderate heat, constant monitoring, adjusting the amount of fuel, adjusting for the wind, and modifying where you place the meat on the grill were all required. The next grill I had was designed by my husband and hand-built by my brother. It made Betsy look like a stable "set it and forget it" oven by comparison; however, it would put an amazing flavor on ribs. I used those grills together to compete against the best of the best, and though they were a lot of work, we won many trophies on them. Yet there was not one contest in which I cooked with an exact recipe; each cook was different. I learned to adjust the temperature and time for each one, making me a much better cook in the long run. There are a lot of good "competition cooks" on the BBQ circuit now. They can follow a recipe to a tee. But throw a curveball—the real cooks always step up while the "recipe cooks" fall by the wayside. If you want to be an expert, put in your ten thousand hours. If you want to be an excellent backyard cook, follow along with the recipes and I guarantee you'll see some significant improvements in your grilling game.

COOKING WITH FIRE

I was raised in rural Mississippi. Yes, BBQ was a big deal there, even before all the TV shows and "back to our roots" cooking that have made BBQ such a huge commercial success lately. However, that's about where the outdoor cooking for a meal ended. BBQ or grilling out, for my family, was more of a social event than a regular meal. No one had time to tend a smoker for hours unless we were cooking for a special occasion, such as a July Fourth picnic. The people I grew up with and around worked hard, and they ate simply.

My love affair with BBQ didn't happen because I had a long family tradition of it, but rather because I loved competition. BBQ was just a means to an end—it was the substance upon which the opportunity to compete and win was built. If there were a pound cake circuit of competitions with big trophies and arrogant men telling me I couldn't do it, then I'd probably be the pound cake queen right now. Then a funny thing happened: I learned to love cooking with fire.

I have never considered myself a chef. I do, however, consider myself the luckiest cook in the world. I never apprenticed in a great kitchen, and I never cooked by my mother's side, but I learned to cook BBQ through trial and error. BBQ gave me opportunities I never knew existed, and I've tried to expand my horizons ever since. Because of BBQ, I've met some great people and worked with talented chefs. Because of BBQ, I've traveled the world and tasted some exquisite dishes, whether in Michelin Star restaurants or humble shacks.

Naturally, from fanning the flames of BBQ grills, I also learned to love just cooking with fire—pure, unadulterated fire. There is something intrinsically honest, something that touches our base souls, about cooking on a grill.

Fire is wild. It is always looking to expand and take over. You have to control it. You have to master something that doesn't wish to be contained.

Grills

People ask me all the time what I cook on at my house. I have all the grills I'll be talking about, and I use them all. I may use a particular grill because it gives a dish a certain flavor or works well with a particular recipe. Some grills are easier to use in inclement weather. Some sit closer to my patio doors than others, and if I'm having a lazy day, that's a good enough reason to use it. Sometimes I may use one just because it's fun to use!

Grills, Cookers, and Smokers

I could really write an entire book on the different grills, cookers, and smokers available today, and I probably still wouldn't cover all the possible selections. So I'm going to take the easy road and just talk about the types I use.

Gas Grills: I've stated before that I'm not quite the purist when it comes to barbecuing and grilling compared to some people in the industry. I believe that if it makes you happy, then it's okay! Who am I to tell people their belief in what makes great

barbecue is wrong (although I do reserve the right to correct someone for misusing the terms *barbecue* and *grilling;* they are NOT interchangeable!). Gas grills are convenient and, if used properly, can produce great food. I also love rotisserie cooking. There is something wonderful about trussing up a whole chicken on a spit and roasting it.

Charcoal Grills: Even though it is so convenient to hit that button on a gas grill and start cooking, charcoal grills are probably the most common grill available today—and with good reason. They're usually less expensive than the other types, and more versatile, and they produce a great flavor when used appropriately. The lower-end models are fine for any type of grilling. They can even be set up for smoking by using an indirect cooking method, where all the fuel is put on one side of the grill and the meat on the other, preferably with a water pan under the meat or beside it to help with temperature control and moisture. Larger, more expensive models are usually made with heavier-gauge metal, a tighter build to control airflow, and better grates.

Ceramic Cookers: These types of grills are very versatile cookers and should be at least a contender for everyone's backyard. By slightly changing the air intakes, exhaust, and fuel, you can easily smoke at a low and slow rate, turn it into a searing-hot grill, or even create a brick oven–style pizza oven. I highly recommend them for home use as they are about the most versatile cooker available.

Smokers: The evolution of the smoker paralleled the rise in competition barbecue. The ubiquitous "barrel grill" made from a prefabricated piece of pipe or propane tank has morphed into double-insulated high-tech pieces of equipment with built-in water pans (or not) and reverse flow with convection fans. I learned to cook on a barrel grill that was so drafty I had to position it just right to get it to temperature, which it could hold for about three minutes before I had to stoke the fire or reposition the grill. However, at the end of the day, the cooker doesn't matter; it's the cook. Now that being said, I have graduated to some fancier smokers, but they are definitely not a necessity outside the world of competition barbecue unless you are intent on winning the backyard barbecue wars. There are several great smoker companies out there today.

Wet versus Dry Smokers: On the circuit, I continually hear people tout the advantages of their favorite types of smoker, whether it's a water smoker or a dry-heat smoker (and generally they will throw in an insult about the opposing type, just for fun). Frankly, both camps are correct, as both smokers can produce absolutely succulent cuisine. I won my world championships with water smokers (really big water smokers for cooking whole hogs!) and use them frequently today. They have some key attributes such as moisture and temperature consistency that make them great choices. Conversely, I prefer some meats to be cooked on a dry smoker, and I've won many world championships on them as well. It really comes down to a personal preference; don't let anybody tell you otherwise.

TOOLS YOU ABSOLUTELY NEED TO HAVE

Charcoal Starting Tool(s): Why people still use lighter fluid is beyond me. If you are one who practices this, know that you have been properly chastised and pledge that you will never again subject your family and friends to the taste of lighter fluid in their dinner. There are many different types of charcoal starters that will not leave any taste in your food. I generally use a charcoal chimney when I'm starting my larger smokers, as it will light a large amount of charcoal at once. There are also electric starters, all-natural fire-starter briquettes (typically compressed sawdust), and wax starters. All are good and will leave you with a fine start to your fire without the bad aftertaste.

Fat Separator Cup: This helps separate the beefy or porky goodness from rendered fats. In a pinch, use a plastic drink bottle with a cap, pour in the rendered beef or pork juices, put the cap on, and turn upside down. After the fat rises to the top, pour out the good stuff for use in a sauce.

Good Knives: Having good knives does not mean having the most expensive knives, but it certainly excludes the cheapest. I bought knives piecemeal at first and built up my set over time. Generally, one can do just about anything with a 6 or 8-inch chef's knife and/or santoku (my favorite), a 10 or 12-inch slicer, a 3-inch paring knife, and a 6-inch fillet knife or utility knife. Handle the knives before purchasing, as brands will feel different due to the weight of the blade, bolster, and handle. A good knife will feel like an extension of your hand. Keep them sharp, and they will reward you with years of service.

Cheap Cotton Gloves: These are "hot gloves" I wear underneath my nitrile gloves. They allow me to handle hot meats for long periods of time and maintain some degree of touch so I can test the texture of the meat. You can get the fancy silicone mitts or gloves if you want, but I have always preferred cotton gloves when handling meat.

Injectors: When I am injecting meat, I use simple, cheap plastic injection needles 90 percent of the time. You can get larger pump-style injectors, but unless you are moving into cooking whole hogs or a large quantity of meat, there's no need, and many times these larger injectors will negatively impact the meat, as they are too forceful.

Insulated Coolers or Cambro: Cambro is a brand of insulated boxes built to hold sheet pans and metal pans for the restaurant and catering industry. Barbecue folks use them for resting briskets, butts, and ribs for extended periods of time as they hold heat extremely well. A regular cooler will suffice for holding meat; just don't try to rest a brisket in a cooler with your cold drinks.

Immersion Blender and/or Food Processor/Blender: These make short work of vinaigrettes, marinades, sauces, and other emulsions and purées. Plus they're fun to use.

Thermometers/Biotherms: A good-quality fast-reading meat thermometer is essential to producing perfect food, especially for someone who is not a professional cook. Fast-cooking items or meats that need to be cooked past a danger zone, such as chicken, require the use of a thermometer. Always calibrate your thermometer using boiling water (adjusting for altitude, if necessary). I also use the probes to test for tenderness in addition to temperature.

Oven Thermometer: A thermometer that reads the internal temperature of meat while it's cooking on the grill, in the smoker, or in the oven allows you to get a sense of where the meat is during the cooking process while keeping the door closed. (If you're looking, you ain't cooking!) Many pitminders will also have a built-in probe for reading the internal temperature as well as the pit temperature.

Map of the Local Farmers' Market: I always try to support local businesses, artisans, and farmers by frequenting farmers' markets to get locally sourced products. However, buyer beware: I have noticed more and more vendors purchasing products through a restaurant supply company and reselling it (generally produce). Look around for the boxes they use to bring in their products. If they are stamped with a brand or another company's name, that product probably wasn't grown, made, or raised by that vendor. Farmers' markets are great sources for humanely raised meats as well as produce and seasonings and often have a local vendor or two selling some great barbecue. What could be better?

Spice Grinder/Mortar and Pestle: A clean coffee grinder works great as a spice grinder and is fairly inexpensive. For small amounts, I find a mortar and pestle works just as well, plus I can get the spice ground to the exact consistency I want.

Grill Baskets: I keep several sizes of grill baskets at the house and use them often. Generally if I think I can cook something without using one, I always will because this eliminates one more item to clean. However, some foods such as vegetables or fish may benefit from a grill basket, as you can more easily move it to different heat zones without losing the food through the grates or tearing it apart.

Grill Brushes, Tongs, Old Towels, and Elbow Grease: I cannot tell you how many times I have seen people pull up to a barbecue contest with dirty, foul-smelling barbecue smokers and start cooking. It's not "seasoned"; it's filthy. Clean your grills! I once lost a contest because the team next to mine had such a malodorous scent that when one judge visited my booth, they thought it was my area and marked me down. An old adage in the restaurant business is "People eat with their eyes." This means that beautifully prepared and plated foods will whet people's appetite. While I fully believe this is true, I also believe we "taste with the nose." Much of the "flavor" we pick up from foods comes from the aroma and the way our sense of smell integrates with our sense of taste. Great-smelling food will absolutely taste better; bad aromas will dull or negate good flavors. I clean my grill grates before and after every cook. My smokers are fully cleaned after every cook, especially before a barbecue contest.

"Seasoning" a smoker is much like seasoning a cast-iron skillet. Allowing oil to bond to the metal through heat will keep it nonstick and free of rust. However, don't use that as an excuse not to clean it! After cleaning and allowing the smoker to dry, spray it with a good coating of oil and it will remain rust-free.

Proper grilling requires a clean, heated grate. Before placing food on them, always oil your grates with an old towel and a small container of a high heat–threshold oil such as peanut oil. Using tongs, dip the towel in the oil and lightly brush the grates. This will not only help keep foods from sticking and forming a buildup on your grates but also aid in getting professional-looking grill marks.

TOOLS YOU WILL WONDER HOW YOU EVER DID WITHOUT

Restaurant Supply Store Membership: Many larger cities have large warehouse-style stores that carry restaurant equipment and/or food supplies. In general, equipment and supplies made for restaurants will stand up to wear and tear significantly better than products at most retail stores. Many restaurant supply stores also tend to offer hard-to-find spices or foods at a much more reasonable price than your typical grocery store.

Chamber Vacuum: This is one of those expensive takes-up-lots-of-space pieces of equipment that you think you will never get good value out of having. However, it has become integral in my kitchen. If you want to make a foray into sous vide cooking, it is a great tool. I use this for quite a few things, such as vacuum sealing meats for the freezer, packaging trimmed meats to take to a contest, compressing and flavorizing fruit, quickly marinating meats (what may take overnight gets done in 30 minutes), quick pickling, and sealing items such as leftover sauces and freezing them. It's worth the cost alone just to compress watermelon. Truly awesome and fun to use.

Meat Maximizer: This is a forty-eight-blade meat tenderizer with spring-loaded action, commonly called a Jaccard in the restaurant industry, after a leading manufacturer. There are many less-expensive brands available at most kitchen stores. Use this tool by pressing the maximizer along the surface of the meat so the blades cut through it. As the incisions are very small, they are not noticeable, especially after cooking. This takes the place of using a huge meat tenderizer, flailing away at a poor piece of meat and beating it into an unrecognizable pulp. It's great for helping to "push" seasonings into the meat as well, and I use it mainly for this purpose.

Baking Stone: Used in a grill setting, baking stones allow you to get true "brick-oven" flavors and are easy to use and clean.

They can be cumbersome to move around and store, but the results make it worthwhile. I have several sizes that can be used on multiple grills.

Pitminders or Controlled Draft Systems: These are electronic thermostats that operate a fan to help a smoker or grill achieve and maintain a certain temperature. In general they are much better suited for use in smokers, but certain grills, such as a Big Green Egg, respond very well to them. Keep in mind that for a pitminder to be effective, you must have a tightly built grill where you can limit the air intake for the fire to the pitminder fan. If you can do that, a pitminder will help control your grill's temperatures. You still must use good fire-building techniques and control the amount of fuel for them to be effective. I use mine as a babysitter for a few minutes, not as a substitute for running my pits. Another very important note: Take grill temperatures from where your items are cooking, not where the temperature gauge is located. A pit may be 350°F in the middle of the cooking chamber but only 220°F at the grate level. Keep this in mind when cooking any recipe.

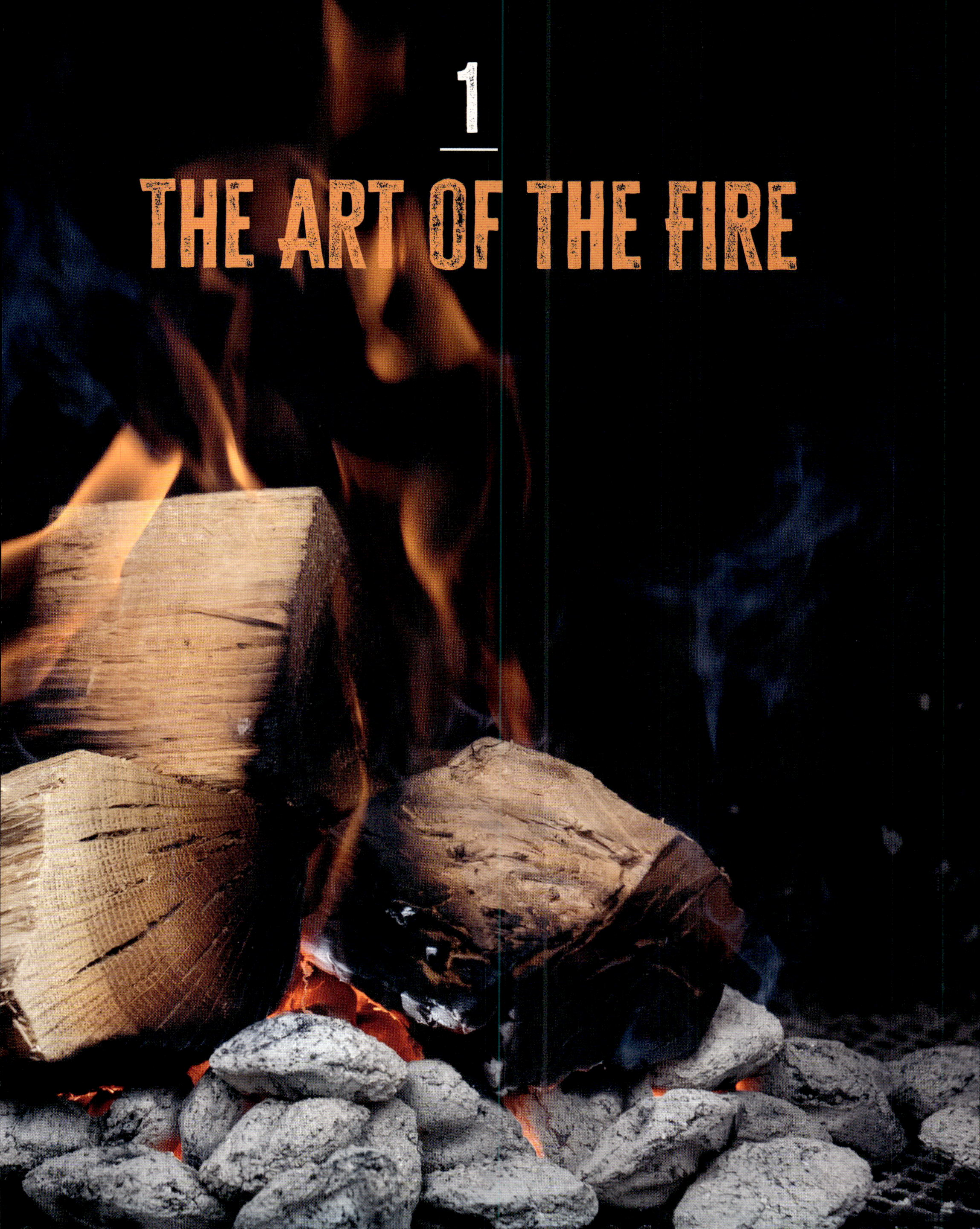

1

THE ART OF THE FIRE

Building a fire is an art unto itself. In a grill situation, where the cooking time is necessarily shortened, the requisite skills aren't as important as the end result. Generally speaking, get the grill hot enough to properly cook your food and you'll be okay. It may not be efficient; you may be burning twice as much fuel as necessary, or the grill may keep burning long into the night after everyone is in bed, but you can get the job done. However, when you want to undertake true barbecue, proper fire building becomes much more important. The food will be exposed to the fire for much longer, so a poorly built fire can easily detract from the flavors of the meat. Also, if the fire is not built correctly, you expend significantly more time, energy, and frustration trying to fix it during the cooking process.

CHARCOALS AND WOODS

Charcoal comes in two main forms: lump and briquettes. Lump charcoal is made of whole pieces of wood that have been exposed to heat in a low-oxygen environment. This smolders the wood and leaves just the carbon. Briquettes are usually made from sawdust exposed to a similar process and then ground and formed into a briquette, along with certain binders to help it keep its form. Lump charcoal tends to be all natural (although I have found plenty of rocks, nails, and the like in bags), while briquettes typically contain additives. Lump charcoal burns hotter and produces less ash, while briquettes burn more consistently and leave you with more to clean up. Lump charcoal, depending on the brand, can help flavor your meat; briquettes usually impart a neutral flavor or no flavor. Lump charcoal needs a much "tighter" cooker to control the airflow to it and manage the heat. Briquettes, by their nature, will burn more consistently in a regular grill. For smoking, I generally start with lump charcoal and then move to briquettes during the middle and later stages.

I use wood for both flavor and heat. I maintain a stockpile of different woods in my garage in both sticks and chunks, and generally keep the following types of wood around:

Apple: Sweet, light flavor and a lighter smoke ring

Cherry: Full, robust flavor that produces a beautiful red smoke ring

Peach: A stronger, more unique flavor than most fruitwood but produces a very light smoke ring

Oak: Neutral flavor and golden-red-hued smoke ring

Pecan: Slightly more intense flavor than oak, with a red smoke ring (one of my favorites)

Hickory: Robust flavor and smoke ring but tends to overpower meats rather quickly; can make meat very dark or black, and can take on bitter overtones (I use it only as an accent wood.)

Mesquite: Can be a nice wood for grilling as it burns very hot and will quickly add some flavor to meats. (Not being from Texas, I am not a fan of smoking with mesquite.)

I have tried many other woods as well. A few of my favorites are pear, persimmon, orange, and walnut, but they are not easily obtainable, so I don't stock them. In addition, several types of wood have multiple subtypes, such as post oak, white oak, and red oak. I listed the main ones as they seem to be the most readily available. I don't worry about using a particular subtype of wood as much as I try to maintain the proper amount of flavor. Keeping your fire burning cleanly and adding wood chunks a few at a time will have far more bearing on how your products taste than the specific type of wood you use.

FIRE BUILDING

Many people, especially novices, think that if some smoke is good, more *must* be better. Nope! First, you must have a clean-burning fire. By this I mean that the fire should be getting enough oxygen to combust properly and have enough flow in and through the grill or smoker to exhaust properly. A smaller, hotter fire is infinitely more desirable than a larger, smoldering fire. You don't get a clean-burning fire by packing an extra bag of charcoal on the fire because it was on sale; you get it by properly igniting and *tending* the fire.

Tending a fire is becoming a lost art in the barbecue world. With the advent of insulated cookers and pitminders, many people have gravitated toward a "set it and forget it" mentality. That is fine and dandy if the weather and wind are perfect, but if you never learn how to properly tend a fire on those occasions when you are "fighting your cooker," you will wish you had. Cooking in the climate-controlled zone of a kitchen, you never have to worry about a passing storm front; temperatures dropping 40 degrees; or rain, humidity, and other factors. But when cooking outside, you almost always will have

to deal with environmental issues that will have an impact on your cooking. The way to overcome this problem is to make sure your fire is built and maintained properly. Keep a smaller fire burning strong. I never soak wood, unless it is chips I am adding to a foil boat to put in a grill. Soaking wood produces a slower, sooty fire and doesn't add a thing to the smoke permeation of the meat. Rather, add a few chunks of wood at a time, allow them to combust cleanly, and add more if needed.

Exhaust maintenance is just as important. You should adjust the smokestack only if there is significant wind, which may be "pulling" the heat out of the cooker. If you are "backing up smoke" in the cooker (that is, smoke is coming out of places it shouldn't), then you need to open the exhaust more or put less fuel on the fire.

I will definitely admit that I use cookers insulated so well, you can set your glass of iced tea on top and not melt the ice. I like to use pitminders, water pans, instant-read thermometers, and any other tool I think will help. However, for years we didn't have any of those items, and I cooked on simple homemade smokers, burning down wood into my own charcoal before putting it in the grill. I have cooked in contests week after week consecutively and used these fancy smokers during the week for catering. Using any smoker that much, I knew exactly what would happen when I would add three chunks of wood or just open the air intake a half inch. All that being said, I still continually fall back on the knowledge of how to build and maintain a fire. Even the best cookers are affected by torrential rains, high winds, and subfreezing temperatures.

A prime example of managing cookers in different weather conditions was at the inaugural Kingsford Invitational in 2012. This contest brought together the winners of the largest and most prestigious barbecue contests of the year, including Memphis in May International Festival, the Jack Daniel's World Championship Invitational, American Royal, and the Houston Livestock Show and Rodeo. Kingsford used a head-to-head judging system to determine the "best of the best." It was held in a field in Belle, Missouri, and the winds were constant and strong during the entire contest. To maintain a given temperature, I had to use significantly more fuel as the wind was pulling the heat out of the cookers quickly. What most people don't realize when this happens is that you get a significant "convection effect," and the items will cook much more quickly than usual as the heat is pulled around your items. I lowered my target temperatures in the cooker slightly to accommodate this, and everything cooked beautifully. I ended up having a pretty good day as well, winning ribs, pork, and brisket and Grand Champion of the event. I know that if I had stuck to my usual cooking time-temperature recipe, I would have severely overcooked some items and had a very mediocre showing.

While there are some who advocate using all wood in their smokers, aka "stick burners," I tend to keep a base of charcoal burning and then add wood for flavor and heat. The specific woods I choose for smoke are as much a tool as a flavoring component. They influence how I build my fire, how I add or lower heat, and how much I use to gently flavor my products. I try to use woods as an accent flavor; it should never overpower the meat. Depending on the item and the smoker, my base fire may be either briquettes or lump charcoal, with hardwood(s) added to the fire.

First, this allows me to keep a more consistent temperature, as charcoal burns more steadily. Second, it allows me to flavor the product as I see fit, adding whatever type or blend of woods that will best accentuate the product I am cooking.

Building a fire in a grill is very similar to building one in a smoker. It needs to be clean-burning. Don't overload it with too much fuel. Direct grilling requires good airflow to achieve the temperatures for searing and cooking.

Direct Heat

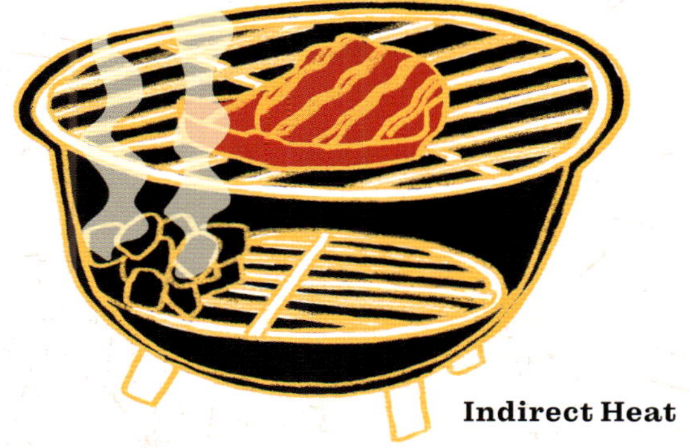

Indirect Heat

SETTING UP A GRILL

There are two main methods of setting up a charcoal or wood-fired grill for home use: the direct method and the indirect method. The direct method is used for straightforward grilling. When you want burgers, hot dogs, and the like, you fire up some charcoal or turn on the burners and start grilling. You have to use enough fuel to generate the heat levels you are looking to get. Place the item directly above the charcoal, and cook to the desired level of doneness.

The indirect method is simply an offshoot of the direct method in that you set all or most of your fire to one side of the grill and cook on the other side so as to have a lower temperature on your items and less chance of charring. In general, setting up a grill for the indirect method is more easily done on a rectangular or larger grill, but it can be done on square, circular, or even small grills. A water pan can be placed on top of the hot side of the grill. This will help blunt some of the heat, add moisture to the cooking chamber, and make your grill temps more consistent. Some people prefer to place the water pan underneath the item being cooked. This method is better if you are adding aromatics such as onions, herbs, juices, or wine to the water pan, as the evaporation of the liquids will help carry some of those flavors up to the meats or vegetables. The classic indirect method is most often used when you are trying to mimic a smoker by putting meat on the cool side and wood and charcoal on the fuel side, thereby achieving lower temperatures on your meat so that you can generate the longer cooking time that some items need.

In this book, where I reference a smoker, you can achieve the temperatures and performance by setting up a grill in this manner. The downside is that it becomes labor-intensive and frustrating to maintain the temperatures needed for a long smoke-cooking recipe. Being more interested in great-tasting food than the purity of the method, I am about to commit barbecue sacrilege with the following statement: Use your oven. Most professional barbecuers wrap their products in aluminum foil or place them in an aluminum pan after a few hours under smoke. This allows the meat to maintain its color profile, limits the smoke flavor, and speeds up the cooking process while not subjecting the meat to the real-world temperature inconsistency when cooking on a smoker. What's the difference between doing that and removing the item from the grill, placing it in a pan or wrapping it in foil, and putting it in your oven to finish? The answer: Not much. Now, when I'm cooking at my house, I like to have a bit more bark and smoke flavor in a pork butt or brisket, so I don't usually wrap them. However, the difference in flavor is a matter of degree, not a wholesale change. There is no shame in keeping a good watch over a pork butt on a grill for three hours to infuse the meat with smoke and flavor, then removing it, wrapping it up, and placing it in the oven at the same temperature. Barbecue is about enjoying life and creating memories, and if your memories involve burned meat, unsuccessful cooks, and feeling too tired to enjoy the fruits of your labor because you've spent eight hours managing a fire every fifteen minutes, then maybe you're doing it wrong.

For most of the grilling recipes, I will reference setting up your grill for two-zone cooking. This is basically a hybrid of the direct and indirect methods, where you are using the majority of your fuel on one side and some of the fuel on the other to create two temperature zones. You can use this to do quite a few things. Most items, such as steak, duck breasts, or even vegetables, benefit from a Maillard reaction, which is the chemical reaction that changes the flavor of food when you brown or sear it. However, to cook to a desired level of doneness, food cannot handle being cooked at a browning/searing temperature for a long enough period without burning. This is where you use a two-zone cooking grid. Brown or sear the product on one side and then move it to the cooler side to finish cooking. Also, when you set a grill up in this manner, you can use it for a variety of functions. I will often sear steaks, move them to a cooler side, and then use the hot side to grill or sauté vegetables, make a sauce in a cast-iron skillet, or grill some fruit for dessert while the steak finishes.

Setting up a gas grill for your desired cooking outcome is even easier, although perhaps not as flavorful. Simply have one side on at a high temp and the other side either off or on a low setting. Adjust the heat on each side until you achieve the desired internal grill temperature. For flavor, a smoker box is an option in many gas grills, or you can wrap some wood chips in foil, poke some air holes in it, and lay it near a burner to smolder. Water pans, with or without aromatics, can be used in a gas grill as well.

HEAT TABLE

These are the "rules of thumb" I use when grilling. Although I don't usually use a thermometer on a grill, this chart equates temperatures to terminology I use in this book.

Searing Heat = 600+°F; used for pizza stones and quick grill marks and sears

High Heat = 500°F to 600°F; used for initial searing, sautéing, and quick-grilling

Medium-High Heat = 400°F to 500°F; general cooking zone
Medium Heat = 350°F to 400°F; used for baking on the grill and finishing items
Medium-Low Heat = 250°F to 300°F; used for finishing items and setting glazes
Low Heat = 250°F to 300°F; used for longer cook time items and braising; smoker temps typically run 225°F to 300°F

I usually check temperatures by holding my hand two to three inches above the cooking grate. On a medium temperature grill, you can usually hold your hand there for six to seven seconds, adding or subtracting two to three seconds for every higher temperature grade. Using this method you can guesstimate the temperature fairly accurately. Most grills and smokers will have a temperature in which where they have different heat levels in different areas of the grill. You can use this to your advantage in cooking. For example, I will place a steak on the hottest part of the grill to gain some quick sear and set my grill marks and then move it to a cooler part to allow the internal temperature to rise to the desired level.

Barbecuers use temperature gradients as well. Even on a well-insulated smoker, there will usually be hotter areas where the heat enters the cooking chamber. These areas can be used to cook different meats, speed up or slow down cooking, develop bark, etc. I use the famous biscuit test when trying out a new smoker to cut down on the learning curve. Simply open a can of biscuits and lay them out in various parts of the grill. Some will cook more quickly than others, showing you where the hot spots are. Many barbecuers with dry cookers will place a water pan over the main hot spot to add humidity to the cooking chamber as well as help maintain the temperatures throughout the grill.

ABOUT SMOKE

Speaking of grills is a good time to bring up smoke flavor. Smoke flavor should not be confused with grilled flavor. The classic flavor of a grill is derived when fats or moisture drip from the meats onto hot coals (or hot metal), carbonize, aerosolize, and impart that flavor back into the meat. Smoke flavor is derived from burning hardwood or certain aromatics (grapevine, herbs, etc.), which allows the flavors to imbue the meat. I have said many times (and will continue to say) that smoke flavor should be viewed as an ingredient. Many novice barbecuers believe that more smoke is better. Frankly, that couldn't be further from the truth.

Even in professional BBQ contests, smoke flavor is not the predominant focus of the meat. If it overpowers the meat, the quality of the entry will be reduced. Nobody wants to burp hickory smoke for three days. In addition to overpowering other flavors quite easily, too much smoke can turn your meat bitter, give it "off" flavors, or turn it an unappetizing black color. No true barbecuer loves too much of a smoke flavor, except everybody's backwoods uncle who yells at every BBQ restaurant that he can do better. To your uncle, I'd tell him to cook his oversmoked BBQ at home and enjoy. To everyone else, enjoy the nuance.

The amount of wood you use is not the only factor in smoke flavor. Some grills are designed to burn only wood (stick burners) and still not overpower the meat. Some can overpower it using only a few chunks of wood.

The main reason is airflow. A Jambo Pit (one of the more famous pits for Kansas City Barbeque Society contests) can burn nothing but hickory, but due to the large air intake and exhaust, it moves a lot of air around the product. This can yield a mildly smoked product.

Pellet grills burn 100 percent wood pellets (compressed sawdust), yet one of their detractions is a lack of smoke flavor. This is due to the pellets' ability to fully combust, burn, and leave little ash. Many "pellet heads" have an auxiliary smoke device to help impart a smoky flavor or are just left with a cooked, grilled product. To get a smoky flavor on a pellet grill, cook at around 225°F or lower, or use an auxiliary smoke flavor device like a smoke tube or a smoker box. Cooking at temperatures around 250°F and above, the pellets will thoroughly incinerate without imparting a smoke flavor to your meats. However, some of the newer models of pellet grills work on a model that imparts more of a smoke flavor than the older units.

Cooking temperature plays a huge part in this equation as well. Cooking a pork butt the low and slow way at 225°F for fourteen hours will yield significantly more smoke flavor than if you cooked it at 275°F for seven to eight hours. Wrapping meat in foil partway through the cook will also decrease the smoke flavor.

We often overlook how much our sense of smell affects our ability to taste. You must realize that, as the cook, you are automatically disqualified from tasting the smoke flavor. When you have your head in a cooker or you are getting a good cloud of smoke in your face, your palate will cease to be able to taste much of a smoke flavor. The next time you cook something, wrap some leftovers in plastic wrap, then smell and taste them in a day or two. I guarantee you will be amazed by their smoky smell and flavor.

We all must realize that BBQ is a very personal food. Some people don't like it unless it has a strong smoke flavor that would overwhelm others. If you love a super heavy smoke flavor, I'll show you some tips to increase it (or decrease it, if you are like me and like a nuanced flavor).

THE PITMASTER'S PANTRY

I have found that most aspiring pitmasters fall into two categories, both of which can be categorized by a peek into their pantry. The first type will have somewhere between ten and twenty-five different commercially prepared barbecue seasonings, sauces, etc. They tend to concentrate on the cooking aspect as opposed to the seasoning aspect of grilling and barbecue. The second type will have as many esoteric salts, herbs, sweeteners, and seasonings as you can count. These people focus on creating their own blends and flavors for seasonings, sauces, marinades, and injections. While I have no problem with the former, I have always counted myself among the latter. This results in a pantry cleanout day about once per quarter as I have to clean out and organize out-of-date spices, mistakes, and impulse buys.

The truth is you can make seasoning blends, sauces, and whatever else that will be just as good as or better than anything you can purchase. This does not mean that you have to have a pantry with every spice known to mankind. Here's a list of items that I use in this book, along with a few other items that I think are important. This is not an all-inclusive list, nor is everything on it a must-have. (Well, a few, such as salts and peppers, are.)

SPICES AND AROMATICS

- Kosher salt, table or iodized salt, sea salt, and flaked or finishing salts
- Black peppercorns, white peppercorns, pink peppercorns, and green peppercorns in brine
- Whole fresh garlic bulbs, garlic cloves, minced garlic, and shallots
- Sweet onions, white onions, red onions, and scallions (green onions)
- Dried chiles: chipotle, ancho, chile de árbol, pasilla, and guajillo
- Chili powders: a medium or light, a hot (generally "dark"), and paprika
- Granulated garlic and granulated onion
- Dried herbs, cumin seeds, coriander seeds, mustard seeds, celery seeds, and fennel seeds
- Fresh herbs: basil, sage, and rosemary (these are especially easy to keep alive in a small herb garden), tarragon, thyme, oregano, cilantro, and Italian (or flat-leaf) parsley
- Jalapeños, poblanos, red and green bell peppers

OILS, VINEGARS, AND OTHER ACIDS

- Fresh lemons, oranges and limes (I love Meyer lemons!)
- Extra-virgin olive oil
- Other oils: peanut (which stands up to a grill and has a neutral flavor); grape-seed, canola, or other high-smoke-point oils are interchangeable
- Balsamic vinegar: good balsamics for drizzling over food or as a dipping oil; less-aged ones for use in recipes and reductions
- Other vinegars: red wine, white wine, cider, citrus champagne, and flavored vinegars

SWEETENERS

- Turbinado sugar, white sugar, light and dark brown sugar
- Local single-source honey (Bees are our friends—support your local apiarist!)
- Orange blossom honey (awesome on a biscuit)
- Agave syrup
- Molasses (preferably in a can from a local sorghum mill)

OTHER INGREDIENTS

- Self-rising, all-purpose, and bread flours
- Celery, carrots
- Yellow, white, and blue cornmeal (self-rising versions are optional)
- Stone-ground grits (available in most supermarkets, but if you're lucky enough to acquire some from the Original Grit Girl, Georgeanne Ross, in Oxford, Mississippi, don't share them with anyone. Hoard them! Stone-ground grits are to the pallid, bland excuse of a white "breakfast" grit as a Ferrari is to an Edsel.)
- Worcestershire sauce, ketchup, and tomato paste
- Tamarind paste (easier to find than it used to be)
- Good-quality chicken and beef paste for making into stock. (Yes, I know it's better to make my own, and I do make it occasionally and freeze it for later use. But sometimes the hours a good-quality store-bought paste saves me is worth it.)
- BACON! (Because who wants to be without bacon?)

HERITAGE BREEDS, RAISING PIGS, AND THE QUEST FOR THE BEST BBQ

Now, here's where you can make a difference in your BBQ!

I have always had a competitive streak. People ask why I love BBQ contests so much, and my standard line has always been "I'm too old for basketball, and I don't like bowling." If there's an opportunity, I just like to compete. And if there's a competition, I sure want to win. That's why I have spent so much time refining my cooking processes, recipes, and meat selection.

When I first started cooking, there wasn't as much of a "selection" of meat to be had. Mostly what was available was commodity pork raised to grow fast and be lean (well, relatively for a pig) as we were in the throes of "the other white meat" pork days. As people have learned to again appreciate the benefits of heritage breeds, natural fat content, and marbling, the choices for pork have expanded considerably.

Heritage breeds don't grow as fast as "commodity" pork breeds such as Yorkshire, Landrace, or Hampshire. Farmers are

looking for efficient growth and consistent results. The ability to sell pork chops at the grocery stores for a very reasonable price has come somewhat at the expense of flavor and marbling, and, frankly, that's okay. There is a lot of value in today's pork, and I've had some great pork chops that I've simply purchased at the grocery store. Yes, a heritage pork chop *may* be better, but there is always a price associated with the slower-growing heritage breeds. I've been very lucky to have access to some incredible pork, but I still go to the grocery store to pick up pork tenderloins, pork chops, and hams just like everyone else.

I have been lucky enough to be a brand ambassador for Prairie Fresh pork for the past few years. I use their ribs in my restaurant, catering, and mail-order food shipments. They own all their farms and take great pride in the quality of pork they produce.

Some consumers and chefs have pushed for having better pork available. Enter the heritage breeds such as Berkshire, Duroc, and, to a lesser extent, Mangalitsa. Of these, Duroc is the most commonly bred into commercially accessible products. Berkshire, while gaining availability, is still a very niche product. Farmers' markets are the best source I have found for Berkshire cuts or ordering online. If you want to try Mangalitsa, you'd better know a farmer or a chef who has them.

Berkshire hogs are the only breed allowed to be graded into Kurobuta pork in Japan because of their wonderful marbling and deep, rich red color. (All Kurobuta pork is Berkshire, but not all Berkshire is Kurobuta.) Just like a prime-grade steak versus a select-grade steak, the intramuscular marbling and increased fat content of some heritage breeds will keep the product moist and tender through the cooking process.

I started cooking Berkshires for Memphis in May years ago. The increased fat gives you a much larger window of doneness, where the meat will stay moist and tender longer due to the basting effect from the marbling. You can certainly have a great product without using a heritage breed, but you have to be right on the money in your cooking times.

Mangalitsas are the coolest-looking pigs in the world, period. They are woolly, like sheep, and the fat content is amazing. Originally from Hungary, these pigs were bred to be able to handle tough weather and terrain. Their fat layer is amazingly thick and produces an ultra-moist product. However, for competition, it's too thick (I never thought I would say that) and almost overshadows the muscle development. I cooked a 200-pound Mangalitsa, and the meat of the hams were the size of a 130-pound commercial hog.

Other breeds are important as well. The famous black Iberian pig is the only breed used for the famous jamón ibérico de bellota. These cave-cured hams are incredible but can get incredibly expensive!

FOOD TRAVELS

I've always had spring fever for traveling. Unfortunately, it's a four-season urge instead of just spring. I love visiting new cities and countries and exploring their history and culture. My favorite thing to do when visiting new cities is to take a food tour. Generally, this means walking through many areas you want to see and getting excellent food as a bonus. The guides let you know the history of the cuisine and provide a good education about that food.

A food tour of Venice introduced me to *cicchetti,* small tasty bites served at many bars and shops for two to three euros each. A tour in Emilia-Romagna introduced me to *pignoletto,* a unique white wine with tiny bubbles produced in a multigenerational winery that has been in the same family for four hundred years. Touring outside Santiago, Chile, I tasted an orange wine for the first time and had the best red wine vinegar of my life. In Lima, Peru, I made *causa,* a potato dish flavored with ají amarillo peppers, and *tiradito,* thinly sliced raw fish served with *leche de tigre, a* spicy citrus sauce. In Vienna, Austria, I tasted amazing pastries and coffee. In Pueblo and Mexico City, I had the best tortilla soup I've ever had and discovered a newfound love for rich mole sauces. On a market tour in São Paulo, Brazil, I tasted the most amazing fruits, many of which I had never seen before. In Guatemala City I became great friends with Gerardo Vera and Pitro Escaler. Pitro took us on a tour of the central market, where I tasted tacos with chicharrónes and *buche* (stewed pork stomach). Gerardo invited us to his beautiful house, where we had *mandarincello,* which was like limoncello but made with mandarin from the trees in his backyard. He also showed us his skills as a pizzaiolo by turning out excellent pizzas from his hand-built wood-fired pizza oven. Maria-Laura Giorgi has taken me on several tours in Rome for touring and food exploration. Artichokes *alla romana* from a restaurant in the Jewish quarter were delicious, as were the *suppli,* a fried rice croquette made with risotto and mozzarella.

In addition to discovering rich flavors and unique preparations that only locals know, you'll generally find the best restaurants, tips and tricks for getting around to the best spots, and learn to appreciate how the geography of an area shapes the cuisine and is the very identity of these places.

WHAT'S FOR DINNER?

Many of the recipes in this book will contain a spice blend or sauces that work well with that dish. However, I often find myself in the mode of "What's for dinner?" My husband is no help in this matter, and we will banter back and forth for hours, until dinnertime is long past, and we decide on a ham sandwich. There's nothing wrong with a ham sandwich; they're pretty tasty, but the few nights we get to have dinner together, I feel we should be *cooking* a meal instead of settling for something else. (Also, not to go on a rant or anything, but grocery-store bread is not very fresh anymore.)

I try to avoid that fate by preparing a few things to have around the house, notably some spice blends, occasional sauce, or the ingredients to make one quickly. For example, one of my favorite seasoning blends is my SPG+ rub, aka Grillin' Shake in my line of consumer-packaged goods. I like it on pork chops or chicken, whether grilled or cooked in a kitchen. So I know I can always pull out a chicken breast, season it up, grill it quickly, and serve it with a salad, and—boom!—dinner is served!

In my childhood, side dishes were often the main course. Even today, I'll have meals with just different side items, and they're among my favorites. Many side recipes accompany an entrée recipe, but don't be afraid to mix and match. As I said, I am not a traditionalist. I believe that whatever tastes good to you is what you should cook (with some occasional experimentation, at least!).

These recipes have been years in the making and are a product of my blood, sweat, tears, and lots of BBQ sauce. They're all-encompassing of my experiences, my travels, and my memories. I hope you enjoy them all.

2

APPETIZERS/SALADS

GRILLED CAESAR SALAD WITH CHILI POWDER CROUTONS

SERVES 4

Chili Powder Croutons

- 1 teaspoon ancho chili powder
- 1 teaspoon salt
- ½ teaspoon black pepper
- 2 tablespoons olive oil
- 2 cups torn or cut bread (such as Italian or French) in 1-inch pieces

Caesar Dressing

- 1 (2-ounce) can anchovy fillets in oil, drained
- 4 cloves garlic, peeled
- 2 large egg yolks
- 2 teaspoons Dijon mustard
- ¼ cup freshly squeezed lemon juice, about 1 to 2 large lemons
- 1 teaspoon coarsely ground black pepper
- ½ teaspoon kosher salt
- ½ cup olive oil

Grilled Romaine

- 4 romaine lettuce hearts, stems intact (or whole heads of romaine, tough outer leaves removed)
- ½ cup olive oil
- Freshly grated Parmesan, for serving

Sometimes I think my life was better when I could enjoy Caesar dressing without knowing that anchovies were what gave it such a wonderful umami flavor. Ignorance can be bliss! The anchovies are optional in this recipe, but you won't technically have Caesar dressing if you omit them. Lightly grilling the romaine gives an unexpected contrast in warmth and allows it to pick up some flavor from the grill. I love putting different textures together or using temperature in unexpected ways, so this salad fits the bill for me.

To make the croutons, preheat the oven to 375°F. In a small bowl, mix together the chili powder, salt, pepper, and olive oil. Spread the bread pieces on a baking sheet and drizzle with the olive oil mixture, then toss to coat all sides. Bake for 10 to 12 minutes, tossing after 5 minutes, until golden brown on all sides. Remove from the oven and let cool.

To make the dressing, place the anchovy fillets, garlic, egg yolks, and mustard in a blender and pulse to combine. Add the lemon juice, pepper, and salt and pulse to incorporate. With the blender running on low, slowly pour in the olive oil to form an emulsion. Place the dressing in a small bowl until ready to serve.

To prepare the lettuce, preheat the grill to medium heat. Brush the outer romaine leaves with the olive oil, then place on the grill, rotating the lettuce so all sides get marked, just until nice grill marks form, about 1 minute per side.

To serve, separate the leaves and toss in the dressing. Arrange on a platter and top with the croutons and Parmesan.

SMASHED CUCUMBER SALAD

SERVES 4 TO 6

- **8 small Persian cucumbers, or 2 English cucumbers**
- **1 tablespoon kosher salt**
- **1 small red onion, thinly sliced**
- **1 teaspoon sugar**
- **2 tablespoons sherry vinegar or rice wine vinegar**
- **1 teaspoon finely minced garlic**
- **2 tablespoons Champagne Mustard (page 47)**
- **1 teaspoon red pepper flakes**
- **1 tablespoon olive oil or sesame oil**
- **1 tablespoon thinly sliced green onion (both green and white parts)**
- **Handful of torn dill or basil leaves**
- **2 teaspoons smoked chili crisp (optional)**

In the summer, it gets so hot in Mississippi that there are days when I eat nothing but cucumber salad for dinner. Luckily, this dish is versatile, and this is one of my favorite versions. You'll want to use Persian or English cucumbers as they're milder and have a thinner skin and fewer seeds. If you like a bit of kick, throw in a dollop of your favorite chili crisp. Trust me, it's delicious.

Halve the cucumbers lengthwise. If using Persian cucumbers, place a half cut side down on a cutting board and lightly smash with the flat side of your chef's knife. You'll want the cucumber to be slightly flattened but not completely smashed. Cut crosswise into bite-size pieces. Repeat with the remaining halves. If using English cucumbers, cut them into bite-size pieces before flattening.

Place the cucumbers in a bowl with the salt and stir to cover all the pieces. Let sit at room temperature for 15 minutes, then discard any liquid released from the cucumbers. Add the remaining ingredients and the chili crisp, if using, and toss to coat. Chill for 20 to 30 minutes in the fridge before serving.

BBQ SHRIMP

SERVES 4 TO 6

- 1 pound jumbo shell-on and head-on whole shrimp, deveined (around 12 per pound)
- 1 tablespoon avocado oil
- 4 teaspoons Delta Creole Seasoning (page 37), divided
- ¼ cup Melissa Cookston Woo Woo Sauce or Worcestershire sauce
- Juice of 2 lemons, about ⅓ cup
- 1 teaspoon Smoke-Roasted Garlic (page 46) or minced garlic
- 1 teaspoon coarsely ground black pepper
- Kosher salt
- ½ cup (1 stick) unsalted butter, cold
- Grilled lemons, for serving
- Loaf of hot crusty bread, for serving

BBQ shrimp aren't actually barbecued at all. They are generally sautéed in a blend of butter, Worcestershire, and spicy Cajun seasoning and served with a piece of French bread for dipping in the flavorful sauce. I prefer to use head-on shrimp for presentation and flavor in this version. If you can't get head-on shrimp, use good domestic large shrimp (16–20 count, or 21–25 count per pound for headless shrimp). To devein shrimp, use a knife to slice down the back of the shrimp's body and remove the vein. I also remove the antennae. If you prefer to remove the heads, place them in a freezer bag and freeze to make an excellent flavored oil or stock later.

Now, while traditional "BBQ Shrimp" are sautéed, you can add even more pop to this already flavorful dish by grilling the shrimp and then topping them with the sauce. If you're looking for a faster meal or don't want to fire up a grill, you can cook the dish entirely on the stovetop.

Soak four thin wooden skewers in water for 30 minutes. Place the shrimp in a mixing bowl and toss with the avocado oil and 2 teaspoons of the seasoning to coat. Thread the shrimp on two skewers so the shrimp won't rotate around the skewers. Refrigerate until you are ready to grill.

Place the Woo Woo Sauce, lemon juice, garlic, the remaining 2 teaspoons of the seasoning, pepper, and salt to taste in a large saucepan over medium heat. Whisk in the butter 1 to 2 tablespoons at a time, waiting until each addition is melted and incorporated.

Preheat a grill to medium heat. Place the shrimp on the grill and cook for about 1½ minutes per side, or until opaque. Remove the shrimp from the grill, pull them from the skewers, and place them in a large serving bowl. Pour the sauce over the shrimp and allow them to sit for 2 to 3 minutes so they absorb the flavor. Serve with grilled lemons and bread.

GRILLED OYSTERS WITH ANCHO BASIL BUTTER

SERVES 4 TO 6

- **1 pound rock salt**
- **½ cup (1 stick) salted butter, softened**
- **1 tablespoon minced fresh Italian parsley leaves**
- **1 tablespoon minced fresh basil leaves**
- **1 tablespoon ancho chili powder or chipotle powder**
- **1 teaspoon minced shallot**
- **1 teaspoon finely grated lemon zest**
- **1 teaspoon kosher salt**
- **1 dozen fresh oysters in the shell, scrubbed, then shucked and on the half shell**
- **Lemon wedges, for serving**

While I'll always love a fresh raw oyster served with extra-spicy horseradish, grilling oysters is a tasty change of pace. I made the ancho basil butter at home and brushed it on crab legs, and I loved it so much that I used it on grilled oysters, too. I recommend trying it, but any flavorful compound butter will also work.

Preheat a grill to medium-high heat. (You'll want some flames for this one.) Place the rock salt in a half sheet pan with a lip.

Combine the butter, herbs, ancho chili powder, shallot, lemon zest, and salt in a microwave-safe container. Place the shucked oysters on the pan, balancing them to keep as much liquid as possible with the oyster. Put approximately ½ tablespoon of the butter mixture on each oyster, then melt the remaining butter mixture in the microwave.

Place the oysters directly over the flames on the grill. Cover the grill and cook for 4 minutes. Open the lid and use a basting brush to drizzle the oysters with some of the butter mixture. (I like letting the flames come up for about 1 to 2 minutes to scorch the shells and slightly increase the grill flavor.) Carefully place the oysters back on the pan and serve with lemon wedges.

SAVORY CROSTATA WITH MELTED LEEKS, GUANCIALE, AND GOAT CHEESE

SERVES 2 TO 3

Dough

½ cup (1 stick) salted butter, cold

1½ cups all-purpose flour

Pinch of salt

¼ cup ice water

Filling

4 tablespoons (½ stick) salted butter

4 to 5 leeks, chopped, white part only

2 teaspoons chopped fresh tarragon leaves

Pinch of salt

Freshly ground black pepper

¼ pound guanciale, cut into strips or matchsticks

2 tablespoons Champagne Mustard (page 47)

6 ounces goat cheese, crumbled

For assembly

1 egg, beaten (for egg wash)

1 tablespoon chopped fresh chives, for garnish

1 tablespoon grated pecorino or Parmesan, for garnish

Guanciale, or cured pork jowl, is a yummy alternative to bacon. Here I think it pairs nicely with the creaminess of the goat cheese and the savory sweetness of the melted leeks. Guanciale fat is liquid gold, so I highly recommend parcooking it by rendering some of the fat in a pan before adding it to the crostata.

To make the dough, cube the butter and place it in a food processor. Add the flour and salt and process until the mixture resembles fine breadcrumbs. (If you don't have a food processor, work the mixture by hand in a mixing bowl.) While continuously mixing, add the water and process until a smooth ball forms. Wrap the dough with plastic wrap and chill for 30 minutes. Line a sheet pan with parchment paper. Roll the dough into an 11-inch circle and place it on the pan.

To make the filling, preheat the oven to 375°F. Melt the butter in a saucepan over medium heat. Add the leeks, tarragon, salt, and pepper to taste, and sauté for 10 to 12 minutes, or until the leeks are tender and slightly brown. Transfer the mixture to a plate. Add the guanciale to the pan and let render, 3 to 4 minutes, being careful not to overcook.

Spread the Champagne Mustard over the dough, leaving 1½ inches of space around the edge. Spread the leek mixture on top, then add the goat cheese and guanciale. Fold the edges up over the filling and pleat. (Your pleating does not have to be perfect.) Brush the top of the dough with the egg, and bake the crostata for 35 to 40 minutes, or until golden. Remove from the oven and let cool for 5 minutes. Garnish with chives and pecorino and serve.

FRIED GREEN TOMATOES

SERVES 4 TO 6

- **1 cup buttermilk**
- **1 cup self-rising white cornmeal**
- **¼ cup self-rising flour**
- **1 teaspoon salt**
- **½ teaspoon black pepper**
- **2 to 3 medium green tomatoes, thinly sliced, end slices discarded**
- **½ cup canola oil**
- **Herby Buttermilk Dressing (page 126) or other dipping sauce, for serving**

Green tomatoes have always been a Southern delicacy and have graced many a summer table. The bitterness of the tomatoes cooks out and leaves a wonderful flavor when combined with the texture of the breading.

Pour the buttermilk into a shallow bowl. In a separate shallow bowl, hand-toss together the cornmeal, flour, salt, and pepper. Place a tomato slice in the buttermilk and turn to coat well. Transfer the tomato slice to the cornmeal mix, pressing it gently to cover, and flip to coat both sides. Set the breaded tomato slice on a plate. Repeat with the remaining slices.

Line a plate with a paper towel. Heat the canola oil in a small skillet over medium heat. Place several breaded tomato slices in the skillet and cook for 2 minutes, then flip and cook for 1 minute, or until crisp. Transfer to the plate to drain. Serve with Herby Buttermilk Dressing or your favorite dipping sauce.

DUTCH BABY HUEVOS RANCHEROS

SERVES 3 TO 4

Ranchero Sauce

Makes 2 cups

1 tablespoon extra-virgin olive oil

1 medium yellow onion, diced

1 to 2 jalapeños (or serranos if you like it spicier), seeded and coarsely chopped

3 to 4 cloves garlic, peeled and smashed

1 (14.5-ounce) can fire-roasted tomatoes

1½ tablespoons chopped chipotle in adobo sauce

1 teaspoon dried Mexican oregano

1 tablespoon ancho or dark chili powder

1 tablespoon chipotle powder

1 cup chicken stock

1 teaspoon ground cumin

1 teaspoon crushed red peppers

½ bunch cilantro, stemmed and coarsely chopped

1 teaspoon kosher salt

½ teaspoon coarsely ground black pepper

Juice of 1 lime (about 2 tablespoons)

Zest of ½ lime

Pico de Gallo

Makes about 1 cup

3 Roma tomatoes, diced

1 medium yellow onion, diced

½ green bell pepper, diced

1 jalapeño, seeded and diced, or 1 teaspoon pickled jalapeños (optional)

1 teaspoon kosher salt

1 teaspoon granulated garlic

½ teaspoon black pepper

Juice of ½ lime

Huevos Rancheros

1½ cups cooked black beans

8 ounces chorizo

1 Roma tomato, chopped

Kosher salt and freshly ground black pepper

2 tablespoons butter, salted

4 eggs

Dutch Baby Pancake

3 large eggs, at room temperature

¾ cup milk, at room temperature

3 tablespoons unsalted butter, melted

½ cup all-purpose flour

2 tablespoons cornstarch

½ teaspoon kosher salt

½ teaspoon black pepper

1 teaspoon minced fresh oregano leaves

½ cup minced fresh Italian parsley leaves

For assembly

2 tablespoons salted butter

1½ tablespoons crema, for drizzling

1 avocado, peeled and sliced, for garnish

2 tablespoons fresh cilantro leaves

2 tablespoons Cotija or queso fresco, for garnish

I love Dutch baby pancakes. They are so versatile. You can serve them for any meal and make them sweet, savory, or even spicy. Dutch baby pancakes are baked instead of cooked on the griddle. I think they are more similar to Yorkshire pudding than a regular pancake.

While traveling in Guatemala, my husband had a version of huevos rancheros with black beans that he liked. This is a take on that but using a Dutch baby pancake instead of the traditional corn tortillas. This recipe features an easy pico de gallo and ranchero sauce. While I much prefer this with the pico de gallo, you can substitute a fresh tomato salsa to help reduce the prep time. Ranchero sauce will keep in the fridge for up to 1 week. Pico de gallo is good for 2 to 3 days in the refrigerator, so you can make both sauces ahead of time to save on prep time. Even the black bean–chorizo mixture can be made a day or two beforehand and then reheated when ready to serve this dish.

To make the ranchero sauce, heat the olive oil in a 2-quart saucepan over medium-high heat, then add the onion and jalapeños. Cook for 5 to 6 minutes, or until softened, then add the garlic and cook for 2 minutes. Add the remaining ingredients except the lime juice and zest, bring to a boil, then decrease to a simmer for 20 to 25 minutes, stirring occasionally, to thicken the sauce. Stir in the lime juice and zest, then use an immersion blender or a food processor and purée until smooth. Store in the fridge until ready to use, for up to 1 week.

To make the pico de gallo, first place the Roma tomatoes in a fine mesh strainer to drain for 10 minutes. Then combine all the ingredients. Let sit for 10 to 15 minutes in refrigerator to enhance the flavor.

To make the huevos rancheros, drain and rinse the black beans. Place the chorizo in a skillet over medium-high heat and break up and brown, about 10 minutes. Add the black beans, Roma tomato, and salt and pepper and cook for 5 to 7 minutes, or until hot.

Place the butter in a separate pan, add the eggs, and cook them according to your taste. (Traditionally, they would be served sunny-side up, but I prefer scrambled.)

To make the Dutch baby pancake batter, blend the eggs in a blender or food processor on medium to high speed for 1 to 2 minutes, or until very frothy. Reduce the blender speed to low and gradually stream in the milk until combined. Then add the butter, flour, cornstarch, salt, pepper, oregano, and Italian parsley, and blend on medium speed for 30 seconds to just combine.

To assemble, preheat your oven or grill to 450°F. Melt the butter in a 10-inch cast-iron skillet and let sit in the center of the oven or grill for 3 to 4 minutes. Remove the warm skillet from the oven and pour in the batter. Place the skillet back in the center of the oven and bake for 25 minutes or until the pancake is puffed and browned on the top, being careful not to open the oven for the first 15 minutes of baking (it might deflate). When it is close to being done, heat the chorizo–black bean mixture. Place the mixture around the Dutch baby pancake, then top with the eggs. Add the pico de gallo, then drizzle the ranchero sauce and crema over the dish. Garnish with avocado, cilantro, and Cotija, and serve.

BLOOD ORANGE ROSEMARY MARMALADE AND FLUFFY BUTTERMILK BISCUITS

SERVES 6

Marmalade

Makes 6 half-pint jars

- 2 pounds blood oranges or Cara Cara oranges
- 1 lemon, finely zested and juiced (about ¼ cup)
- ⅓ cup water
- 4 cups sugar
- 1 tablespoon finely chopped fresh rosemary
- 1 teaspoon kosher salt

Buttermilk Biscuits

Makes 10 to 12 biscuits

- ½ cup (1 stick) unsalted butter, cold
- 1 teaspoon kosher salt
- 4 cups self-rising flour, chilled
- 1½ cups Bulgarian-style buttermilk, cold

I grew up spending the summers with my grandparents on their farm. Every morning, I would watch them make breakfast: two pieces of toast with homemade orange marmalade and a fried egg. This marmalade recipe holds fond memories for me. I'm more a fan of biscuits than toast, so nowadays I pair my marmalade with a fluffy biscuit. My grandparents probably ate toast because my grandmother was certainly not the best biscuit baker in town; they had a good flavor but resembled manhole covers more than biscuits. (Don't worry, this biscuit recipe isn't hers.)

The real trick to a good fluffy biscuit is to keep the cold ingredients very cold. I chill the ingredients between steps before placing them in the oven. It's not a requirement, but doing so enhances the fluffiness factor. Another thing I use in my kitchen is Bulgarian-style buttermilk. It's a cultured buttermilk that is thicker and tangier than regular buttermilk, and it improves biscuits, dressings, cornbread, and other buttermilk-based items.

(continued)

To make the marmalade, very thoroughly scrub the oranges and cut off the ends. Quarter the oranges and discard the seeds. Place them in a food processor and process until the rind is in very small pieces. Then place the oranges in a large saucepan over medium heat and add the lemon zest and juice, water, and sugar. Bring to a boil over medium-high heat. Decrease the heat to low and simmer for 35 to 40 minutes, until thickened. When the marmalade is ready, it will slide off a spoon in sheets. Mix in the rosemary and salt and cook for 1 minute. Let cool, then store in jars or a container. The marmalade will keep in the fridge for 3 to 4 weeks.

To make the biscuits, very lightly grease a large cookie sheet, or, for a crispier crust, use a cast-iron skillet.

Cut the butter into small cubes or, even better, grate it. Place the butter, salt, and flour in a large mixing bowl and cut the butter into the flour using a pastry cutter. (Or place the butter, salt, and flour in a large food processor and pulse until coarse crumbs, like rough cornmeal, form.)

Refrigerate the flour mixture for 20 to 30 minutes. (If you used a food processor, transfer the mixture to a mixing bowl before refrigerating.) Then form a well in the middle of the mixture and pour in the buttermilk. Using a plastic spatula, fold the mix until a rough dough forms. (Be careful not to overmix.)

Turn the dough onto a lightly floured surface and, with floured hands, press it into a ¾-inch-thick rectangle. (The dough will be sticky, so have some extra flour nearby.) Cut the dough in half and put one half on top of the other. Turn the dough 90 degrees and press it back into a ¾ to 1-inch-thick rectangle.

Complete this process 3 or 4 times to help generate layers in the biscuits. Leave the dough 1 to 1¼-inch thick for the final press into a rectangle. Using a sharp biscuit cutter, cut directly into the dough without twisting or sawing, as that will impede the sides from properly flaking. After cutting the dough, lightly form the remaining dough into a rectangle. Place the biscuits on the cookie sheet at least 1 inch apart and put them back in the fridge for 10 minutes.

Preheat the oven to 475°F. Bake the biscuits for 12 minutes or until golden brown. Serve with the marmalade.

PROVOLETA WITH CHIMICHURRI AND ROASTED CHERRY TOMATOES

SERVES 4

Chimichurri

Makes 1 cup

1 bunch Italian parsley, stemmed and coarsely chopped

1 bunch cilantro, stemmed and coarsely chopped

1 tablespoon coarsely chopped fresh oregano leaves

2 to 3 cloves garlic, peeled and smashed

1½ tablespoons red wine vinegar

1½ teaspoons kosher salt

¾ teaspoon black pepper

1 teaspoon red pepper flakes

½ cup extra-virgin olive oil

Provoleta

1 teaspoon olive oil

10 to 12 cherry tomatoes, skewered, brushed with olive oil, and lightly sprinkled with kosher salt

One (1½-inch) thick slice unsmoked provolone (ask the deli counter to cut it this thick)

Crusty bread or pita chips, for serving

Provoleta is an Argentinian comfort dish of ooey-gooey melted *provoleta* cheese, which unfortunately isn't readily available in the States. Provolone, which *is* available, is a close cousin and will work well for this recipe. Provoleta can be prepared as simply as melting provolone but is generally topped with seasonings, chimichurri, or other items to amp up the flavor.

Like chermoula (page 120), chimichurri is an herbaceous sauce that complements almost any grilled item. When my herb garden is producing, I always keep this sauce in my fridge, as it is so simple to lightly season a piece of fish, chicken, or steak, grill it, and top it with chimichurri.

I also like to roast some cherry tomatoes to serve with this dish, giving it some tomato umami that blends well with the melty cheese and chimichurri. Serve this with toasted crostini, warm crusty bread, or pita chips.

For best results, use a 6-inch cast-iron skillet to melt the cheese. The cast iron will heat evenly and then retain heat to help keep the provoleta at maximum cheese-pull goodness.

Provoleta is typically made on a grill while meats are cooking. You can make this in the oven (preheat to 400°F, cook until melted, then broil until bubbly and browned), but I prefer to place it on a grill as an appetizer before I add it to the main dish.

(continued)

To make the chimichurri, place all the ingredients except the olive oil in a food processor and pulse to combine. While processor is running, drizzle in the olive oil. Taste and adjust the seasoning as needed. Set aside until ready to serve. The chimichurri will keep in the fridge for up to 1 week.

To make the provoleta, pour the olive oil into a cast-iron skillet. Prepare a grill to medium-hot with a two-zone fire, and place the skillet on the warmer side for 10 minutes to preheat.

Place the cherry tomatoes on the hot side of the grill to char for about 2 minutes per side. Then move the tomatoes to the cooler side of the grill to finish roasting.

Place the provolone in the hot skillet and cook for 45 seconds to 2 minutes, or until the edges begin to melt. Using a metal spatula, flip the provolone and cook for 6 to 8 minutes, until the provolone is bubbly and melty. Remove the skillet from the grill, top the provolone with the chimichurri and the tomatoes, and serve with bread or pita chips.

SPICY SPINACH CRAB DIP

SERVES 6 TO 8

- **Olive oil, divided**
- **½ medium yellow onion, minced**
- **3 cloves garlic, peeled and grated**
- **12 ounces fresh baby spinach**
- **2 serranos, seeded and diced**
- **1 (8-ounce) package cream cheese**
- **⅓ cup torn fresh mozzarella**
- **¼ cup grated fontina**
- **8 ounces lump or special crabmeat**
- **2 teaspoons lemon zest**
- **1 tablespoon Delta Creole Seasoning (page 37)**
- **1 teaspoon smoked paprika**
- **Kosher salt and freshly ground black pepper**
- **2 to 3 slices white bread**
- **Pita chips or toasted bread, for serving**

Like Martin Short's character in *Only Murders in the Building,* I could exist on dips. I like ranch, hummus, queso, salsa, and anything else you can make into a dip. This recipe is for a hot dip, and it's delicious. You can make this without the crabmeat and have a delicious spinach and artichoke dip, or substitute shredded chicken, grilled chopped shrimp, or even pulled pork.

Heat a saucepan over medium heat, add a drizzle of the olive oil and the onion, and cook until the onion is translucent, 3 to 4 minutes. Add the garlic and cook for about 1 minute.

Add the spinach a handful at a time and continually stir as it wilts, then add the next handful and repeat. Sauté until the moisture from the spinach has evaporated.

Add the serranos and cream cheese, and stir to combine. Lower the heat, and gradually fold in the mozzarella and fontina a bit at a time. Continue to cook and stir until all the cheese has melted. Add the crabmeat, lemon zest, seasoning, paprika, and salt and pepper to taste. Transfer the dip to an oven-safe dish.

Preheat the oven to 400°F. Place the bread and ½ tablespoon olive oil in a food processor and pulse until the bread forms small breadcrumbs. Layer the breadcrumbs on top of the crab dip and bake for 15 to 20 minutes, until the top is golden brown. Serve with pita chips or bread.

3

SAUCES/SEASONINGS

CLASSIC BBQ SAUCE

MAKES ABOUT 6 CUPS

¼ cup canola oil
¾ cup finely diced sweet or yellow onion
2 tablespoons minced garlic
1½ cups ketchup
½ cup honey
2 tablespoons tomato paste
¼ cup white vinegar
¼ cup plus 2 tablespoons packed dark brown sugar
¼ cup Worcestershire sauce
2 teaspoons dry mustard
1 teaspoon cayenne pepper
1 teaspoon black pepper
½ cup water, or as needed
½ cup Classic BBQ Rub (page 38)

This recipe has always been our "mother" competition sauce—the base we use to make the sauces we serve for competition judges. It is very forgiving of tweaking, so use it as a palette to get creative! One of my favorite variations is to add a cup of my peach syrup (that I bottle and sell) or some muscadine jelly to the base. When cooking competition chicken, I leave out the diced onion and substitute 1 tablespoon of onion powder as I like a smoother finish on chicken.

In a medium saucepan, heat the canola oil over medium heat. Add the onion and sauté until translucent, about 5 minutes. (Decrease the heat to low if the onion is cooking too fast; you don't want it caramelized or browned.) When the onion is almost translucent, add the garlic and cook until lightly golden, about 2 minutes. Add the ketchup, honey, tomato paste, vinegar, brown sugar, Worcestershire, dry mustard, cayenne pepper, and black pepper and stir well. Slowly add the water until the sauce reaches your desired consistency. (A slightly thick consistency is best.) Add about 3 tablespoons of the rub, stir well, and taste. The sauce should have a good, well-rounded flavor. Add the rub in 1-tablespoon increments to taste. Cool and store in an airtight container in the refrigerator for up to 10 days.

DELTA CREOLE SEASONING

MAKE ABOUT ¾ CUP

- **2 tablespoons paprika**
- **3 tablespoons kosher salt**
- **2 tablespoons granulated garlic**
- **1 tablespoon coarsely ground black pepper**
- **1 tablespoon onion powder**
- **1 teaspoon cayenne pepper**
- **1 tablespoon dried oregano**
- **1 teaspoon dried basil**
- **1 tablespoon dried thyme**

I use this whenever I want a little more kick in a sauce or whenever I'm bronzing chicken, fish, or pork. It also works great as a barbecue rub for smoked pork tenderloin.

Combine all the ingredients in a small mixing bowl and stir by hand until well incorporated. Store in an airtight container for up to 1 month.

CLASSIC BBQ RUB

MAKES 3 CUPS

- **1½ cups turbinado sugar**
- **½ cup kosher salt**
- **1 tablespoon onion powder**
- **⅓ cup granulated garlic**
- **1½ teaspoons cayenne pepper**
- **1 teaspoon finely ground black pepper**
- **2 teaspoons dry mustard**
- **½ cup light chili powder**
- **1 teaspoon ground cumin (see headnote)**
- **¼ cup plus 2 tablespoons paprika**

This is my world championship—winning tried-and-true rub recipe. I use it on any cut of pork, especially whole hog and ribs. Right before mixing any seasoning blends containing cumin, I like to lightly toast cumin seeds in a clean, dry skillet over medium heat for about 2 minutes, or until aromatic, and then grind them. This brings out the oils and really improves the flavor.

Place the turbinado sugar in a coffee grinder and pulse until lightly powdered. Transfer to a small mixing bowl and add the remaining ingredients. Stir until well incorporated. Store in an airtight container for up to 1 month.

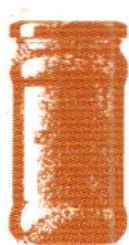

HERBY CULTURED BUTTER

MAKES 12 OUNCES

- **4 cups heavy cream (not ultra-pasteurized)**
- **3 tablespoons plain yogurt**
- **2 teaspoons kosher salt**
- **1 teaspoon chopped fresh basil leaves**
- **1 teaspoon chopped fresh dill**
- **1 teaspoon chopped fresh chives**

I'm not a snob about most things, but I do consider myself a butter snob. In my opinion, butter needs to be cold and, most important, salted. But if you really want to kick butter up a notch, make or buy cultured butter. Cultured butter is made by fermenting cream with bacterial cultures and then churning it as you would regular butter to separate the fat from the buttermilk. The very slightly tangy flavor you get from culturing your butter is so worth the 18 to 24 hours you have to let it ferment—trust me.

Combine the cream and yogurt in a lidded container and stir to ensure the yogurt is evenly distributed. Allow the mixture to sit covered at room temperature for 18 to 24 hours. (The flavor will become more pronounced and tangier as it sits, and it will also thicken with time.) Then transfer the mixture to the fridge and let sit for 1 hour.

Pour the mixture into a food processor and add the salt. Turn on the processor and let it run for about 10 minutes. (The whipped cream will disintegrate and break into liquid and solids.) After it's separated, process for 1 more minute.

Line a fine mesh sieve with a cheesecloth and use it to strain the liquid (the buttermilk) into another container. Press the solids (the butter) between your hands to remove as much liquid as possible. Store the buttermilk to use in other recipes. It will keep in the fridge for up to 5 days.

Transfer the butter to a mixing bowl and wash it repeatedly with very cold water to release any excess buttermilk. Strain the butter and repeat until the liquid is clear, about 4 to 6 washes. (Washing it well will help extend its shelf life.)

Add the herbs to the butter and work with your hands or a wooden spoon to combine. Shape the butter as desired and wrap in wax paper. Store well-wrapped in the fridge for up to 1 month or freeze for up to 6 months.

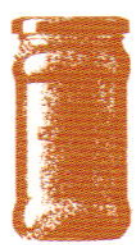

HERB OIL

MAKES 1 CUP

- **2 cups water**
- **2 lightly packed cups of your favorite herb leaves**
- **Ice bath**
- **1 cup olive oil or avocado oil**

Flavored oils are easy to make and can provide beautiful color and flavor to finish dishes. You need only two ingredients: good finishing olive or avocado oil and herbs. You can pick whichever herbs you like or blend them. You can also use this method to make chili oil. I keep at least one herbal oil (usually parsley, basil, or chive oil) on my counter for finishing dishes. Blanching the herbs first will help preserve the rich color of the herb oil.

In a small saucepan, bring the water to a boil. Then add the herbs and stir. Blanch them for 30 seconds, then strain the herbs, discard the liquid, and immerse the herbs in the ice bath. Let sit for 2 minutes, then strain them again. Pat the herbs dry with a paper towel, and place them on a wire rack in a single layer to dry completely, about 1 hour.

Place the olive oil and dehydrated herbs in a blender. Pulse, then blend on high speed for 2 to 3 minutes. Turn off the blender. Line a fine mesh strainer with cheesecloth, place it over a mixing bowl, and pour the oil mixture into the strainer. Strain it for up to an hour, then press the herbs into the cheesecloth with the back of a spatula to release any remaining oil. Store in a jar in the fridge for up to 3 months. Remove from the refrigerator at least 1 hour before using.

SMOKY BEEF TALLOW OR PORK LARD

MAKES 5 TO 6 CUPS TALLOW OR LARD

5 pounds pork or beef fat, cut into 1-inch pieces

Large container of ice water

I trim a lot of external fat when cooking brisket or whole hogs. A 16 to 18-pound brisket will yield about 5 to 7 pounds of fat! I hate wasting things that can be delicious, so I like to make smoky beef tallow with it or save the fat from trimming hogs and make smoky pork lard. Fat can be used in many ways and is a flavorful medium for roasting or frying potatoes, veggies, and much more. It has a higher smoke point than most vegetable oils and adds amazing flavor to your cooking. Generally, 1 pound of fat will yield about 1½ cups of tallow or lard. Cut the fat into small pieces or run it through a grinder to help it render. To make lard, follow the same recipe using pig fat.

You can make tallow on the stovetop or in a slow cooker, but I like to smoke it to add that smoky taste. I usually make it in aluminum pans and then pour the tallow through a strainer before storing it.

Prepare a smoker to cook at 250°F.

Remove any excess meat pieces from the fat, then soak the fat in ice water. (This helps get rid of any blood or other impurities; you can skip this step if you have nice, clean fat.) Strain the fat from the water, place it in a sturdy pan (or doubled disposable aluminum pans), and put the pan in the smoker. (This lets the fat slowly render.) Skim off any scum and discard it as the fat cooks. (If you do the ice water soak, you won't have as much scum to deal with.) Cook for 3 to 4 hours, until most of the fat is rendered. The finished temperature should be 225°F to 230°F. (This ensures that almost all the water will have cooked out.) Very carefully pour the tallow through a fine mesh strainer, then pour into quart jars and freeze for long-term storage or store in the fridge. Tallow or lard will last for several months if fully rendered and stored in the refrigerator. It will last a year or more in the freezer.

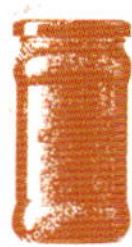

SPG+ SEASONING

MAKES 3 CUPS

- **1 cup kosher salt**
- **1 cup coarsely ground black pepper**
- **½ cup granulated garlic**
- **½ cup smoked paprika**
- **½ tablespoon dry mustard powder**

This is a great "season-all," and I use a derivation of it almost daily. My Grillin' Shake, which I sell, is a version of this seasoning on steroids, and it's great for virtually any grilled meat. Whenever I call for you to "season with salt and pepper," you can use this blend instead. Make this in bulk and keep it in an airtight container for up to 4 months.

Keep this spice blend in your kitchen for quickly seasoning chicken, beef, or pork. And it's eminently customizable. For example, if I'm doing a low and slow brisket, I up the black pepper to give it a darker, peppery crust. I usually increase the dry mustard for pork chops and add a bit of ancho chili powder or cayenne pepper. For the kosher salt, I use Morton's because of the bigger flakes.

Mix together all the ingredients in a mixing bowl. Store in an airtight jar for up to 4 months.

SMOKE-ROASTED GARLIC

MAKES ¼ CUP

1 head garlic
Olive oil

Smoke-roasting garlic adds depth of flavor and is simple to prepare. You can roast the garlic in an oven, but roasting it in a smoker adds even more flavor. It keeps in the freezer or fridge, covered in olive oil, for up to 2 weeks.

Prepare a smoker to cook at 275°F to 300°F. Trim about ¼ inch from the top end of the garlic. Wrap aluminum foil around the bottom and sides, leaving the top exposed. Drizzle with olive oil and place in the smoker for 45 minutes to 1 hour, or until softened. Let cool, then squeeze out that garlic goodness.

CHAMPAGNE MUSTARD

MAKES 1 QUART

- **½ cup yellow mustard seeds**
- **½ cup black mustard seeds**
- **1 tablespoon kosher salt**
- **1 tablespoon honey**
- **1 cup champagne or sparkling wine**
- **½ cup vinegar (I like to use champagne vinegar.)**

Making your own mustard is very easy to do. With this recipe, you can make it to your specifications. I keep this in the fridge and use it in many items—in vinaigrettes, on sandwiches, in recipes, and more.

Place the mustard seeds, salt, honey, and champagne in a quart jar. Let it sit for a few minutes to allow the bubbles to dissipate, then add the vinegar. Seal the jar and let sit at room temperature for 24 to 48 hours.

Pour the mixture into a blender or food processor and process on high until it forms a paste, about 1 minute. The mixture will thicken more the longer it sits. Transfer to a container or jar and cover. The champagne mustard will keep in the fridge for at least 1 month.

SMOKED TOMATO POWDER

MAKES ¼ CUP

2 cups thinly sliced Roma or San Marzano tomatoes or your favorite type of tomato (heirloom cherry tomatoes also work well)

I use this same method to make several dried powders or spices throughout the year. It's very easy and lets you uniquely customize your spice rack. I often make smoked jalapeño powder for a hint of spice in a rub, green tomato powder to add a tart flavor, or ginger, mushroom, or green onion powder. While I generally make single-spice powders, you can also make your own blends this way. The flavor you'll get from dehydrating and grinding your own spices is far better than what you'll get from store-bought spices. Use this powder to flavor up pastas, spice rubs, stews, or soups. I also love to use it to make Tomato-Spiced Beans and Rice (page 123).

Prepare a smoker to cook around 180°F with moderately heavy smoke. For this recipe, I like to use pecan or oak wood; fruit wood also works well.

Lightly coat a wire rack with oil. (I used duck fat spray.) Place the tomato slices in a single layer over the rack and place the rack in the smoker for 2 hours.

Remove the rack, place the tomato slices in a dehydrator, and dehydrate for 18 hours at 121°F. Place the tomatoes in a spice blender and purée into a powder. (You can also place them in a resealable jar to use as sun-dried tomatoes.) Smoked tomato powder will keep for a year or more in a glass jar.

4
PORK

PULLED PORK

MAKES 3 TO 4 POUNDS PULLED PORK, ENOUGH FOR 12 TO 16 SANDWICHES

- **1 (8 to 10-pound) pork butt**
- **1½ cups pork injection**
- **5 tablespoons Classic BBQ Rub (page 38), divided, plus 1 tablespoon (optional)**
- **About ¼ cup mustard, divided**
- **⅓ cup turbinado sugar**
- **½ cup Classic BBQ Sauce (page 36), plus more for serving**

The pork butt is really kind of misnamed. It has nothing to do with what people consider a butt (on a hog, that would be the ham) but rather is the upper portion of the pork shoulder containing the blade bone. (The lower portion is called the picnic and contains more bone and fat.) We cook more than 6 tons of Boston butts a week at my restaurant, Memphis Barbecue Company, so I truly love them. They really become a sublime treat when cooked properly into Memphis-style pulled pork. For the pork injection, I suggest using mine! You can find it at TheBBQAllstars.com.

Place the pork butt, fat side down, in an aluminum cooking pan. Using a small injection needle, inject the butt with the pork injection using a checkerboard pattern. Pour any remaining injection over the butt. Cover and refrigerate for at least 4 hours and up to overnight.

Prepare a smoker to cook at 250°F with cherrywood and applewood. (I love mixing these two woods—about 4 to 6 chunks each—for smoke when I'm doing pork.) Liberally sprinkle 2 tablespoons of the rub on the meat side of the butt, spread about 3 tablespoons of the mustard over the top in a zigzag pattern, and lovingly massage them in. Remove the butt from the pan, place in the smoker, and cook for 4½ hours.

Lay out 2 large sheets of heavy-duty aluminum foil (about 2 feet long) and arrange in a crisscross pattern. Place the butt on the foil and sprinkle with 2 tablespoons of the rub, then spread with about 1 tablespoon of the mustard. Rub in the mustard, then sprinkle with the turbinado sugar. Bring up each piece of foil to fully enclose the butt, return it to the smoker, and cook for 4 to 4½ hours, or until the internal temperature is 195°F. (If you like more "bark" on the pork, open the foil and sprinkle with 1 tablespoon of the rub before the last hour of cooking.)

(continued)

Place the wrapped butt in a pan and poke a hole in the foil to drain the excess grease. Let rest in a Cambro or cooler for 1 to 2 hours.

Wearing heat-resistant gloves, hand-pull the pork apart. Add the remaining 1 tablespoon of the rub and ½ cup of the sauce, and massage them into the pork. Serve with sauce on the side.

What makes a Memphis-style sandwich? Tender pulled pork like this, a rich flavorful sauce like our Classic BBQ Sauce (page 36), and a good helping of coleslaw (page 143) on a good old-fashioned plain bun. (When you see some chefy type trying to sell you a barbecue sandwich on a "hearth-baked onion-sesame brioche bun," you know they're not from Memphis!)

BABY BACK RIBS

SERVES 2 TO 4

- **2 slabs baby back ribs, about 3 pounds each**
- **¼ cup plus 2 tablespoons Classic BBQ Rub (page 38), divided, plus more for sprinkling**
- **¼ cup plus 2 tablespoons yellow mustard, divided**
- **2 tablespoons honey, divided**
- **4 tablespoons turbinado sugar, divided**
- **4 tablespoons purple grape juice**
- **About ½ cup Classic BBQ Sauce (page 36)**

I'm known in the media and among competitors as a whole-hog cook, and I've been very fortunate with whole hogs in contests. However, I've won a lot more contests with my baby back ribs. This recipe won first place in eight contests in a row—a pretty mean feat! These ribs have a full flavor profile: a little sweet, some acid, a little salt, and just enough heat on the back of your palate to make you want another bite.

Rinse the ribs and remove the membrane from the back. Trim any excess fat from the top of the slabs. Trim 1 bone from the large end of the ribs and 2 bones from the small end. (This will give you a much more consistent slab for cooking.)

Starting on the back, sprinkle each slab with about 1½ teaspoons of the rub, then add 1½ teaspoons of the mustard to each and massage into the meat. Flip the ribs over and repeat. Wrap the ribs tightly in plastic wrap and refrigerate for at least 8 hours. (For a contest, I marinate ribs like this for 12 to 16 hours.)

Prepare a smoker to cook at 225°F with about 4 chunks of applewood and 4 chunks of cherrywood so that the wood will smolder throughout the cooking. Unwrap the ribs and repeat the rub-and-mustard procedure. (Don't get it too thick or paste-like, as this will give the ribs a dark appearance when cooked.)

(continued)

Place the ribs in the smoker, meat side up, and cook for 2 hours. Remove the ribs and increase the temperature to 250°F. Repeat the rub and mustard on both sides of the ribs. Slather about 1 tablespoon of the honey on each of the top sides, then on each slab sprinkle heavily with about 2 tablespoons of the sugar. Lay out a large piece of heavy-duty aluminum foil and place the ribs, meat side down, on top. Fold up the edges. Pour the grape juice onto the foil. Finish wrapping the ribs, but don't crimp the edges. (You want steam to be able to escape.)

Return the ribs to the smoker and cook for 2 hours. Open the foil and check for tenderness. (At this stage I cook ribs until they look overdone and too tender. Don't worry; they'll tighten up. If they still have too much texture, leave them in the smoker for another 20 to 30 minutes.) Remove the ribs from the smoker, open the foil, and drain the liquid. Brush a fourth of the sauce on the bone side of each rib. Then, using the foil as a tool, "roll" the ribs over so the meat side is up and brush the top. Using long tongs, carefully remove the ribs from the foil, place them back in the smoker, and cook for 15 minutes. (This will let the glaze cook onto the ribs and let the ribs tighten back up.) Remove the ribs from the cooker and let rest for 5 minutes. Apply a very thin coat of sauce to "glisten" the ribs, then very lightly sprinkle with the classic rub before serving.

For competitions, we ask our meat market to run the ribs through a bandsaw and lightly trim off the double bones and knuckles on the ends. We also trim all the meat and fat from the top of the ribs except for the cross grain that runs across the middle. These steps help create a more consistent size for cooking and improve the appearance. If you are cooking at home, these steps aren't necessary.

PORK SPARERIBS

SERVES 2 TO 4

- **2 slabs St. Louis spareribs, about 3 pounds each**
- **¾ cup Classic BBQ Rub (page 38), divided, plus ½ cup in a shaker with very small holes**
- **¼ cup plus 2 tablespoons yellow mustard, divided**
- **1 cup Italian salad dressing, divided**
- **1 cup packed light brown sugar, divided**
- **½ cup honey, divided**
- **½ cup Classic BBQ Sauce (page 36), divided, plus more for brushing**

Outside Memphis, where baby backs are predominant, spareribs are usually served in most restaurants. Spareribs are cut from the area closer to the belly (bacon) and therefore have a richer, more "porky" flavor than baby backs. We serve St. Louis–cut ribs (spareribs with the breastbone area trimmed off), as they cook more consistently.

Rinse the ribs and remove the membrane from the back. Trim any excess fat from the tops of the slabs. Starting on the back, sprinkle each slab with about 1 tablespoon of the rub, then spread 1½ teaspoons of the mustard on each and massage it into the meat. Flip the ribs over and repeat. Wrap them tightly in plastic wrap and refrigerate for 8 to 12 hours.

Prepare a smoker to cook at 250°F with cherrywood and pecan wood. Unwrap the ribs and repeat the rub-and-mustard procedure, massaging them in. (Don't get it too thick or paste-like, as this will give the ribs a dark appearance when cooked.) Place the ribs in the smoker, meat side up, and cook for 2 hours, using a barbecue mop to lightly baste the tops with the Italian dressing every 30 minutes. Remove the ribs from the smoker and increase the temperature to 275°F.

Apply the rub and mustard to both sides of the ribs as before. Tear off a large sheet of heavy-duty aluminum foil for each slab, and on each sheet, sprinkle ½ cup of the brown sugar in the area where you will put the ribs, then drizzle ¼ cup of the honey and ¼ cup of the sauce over the sugar. Place a slab, meat side down, directly in the sugar mix, then close the foil over the ribs, but don't crimp the edges. (You want steam to be able to escape.)

Return the ribs to the smoker and cook for 2 hours. Open the foil and check for tenderness. The ribs should be tender but still have texture. Remove them from the smoker, open the foil, and drain the liquid. Remove the ribs from the foil and brush the sauce on the bone side of the ribs, then flip over and brush the sauce on the top.

Carefully return the ribs to the smoker and cook for 15 minutes to tighten up the glaze, then remove and let rest for 5 to 10 minutes. Slice the ribs into serving portions, lightly dust with the rub, and serve.

PEPPERED PORK TENDERLOIN WITH HOECAKES AND MISSISSIPPI CAVIAR

SERVES 4

Mississippi Caviar

2 cups drained cooked black-eyed peas

1 cup fresh whole-kernel corn

1 cup diced tomato

1 tablespoon diced jalapeño (optional)

1 tablespoon chopped fresh cilantro leaves

1½ teaspoons canola oil

½ teaspoon kosher salt

¼ teaspoon granulated garlic

½ teaspoon ground cumin

Pork

2 teaspoons coarsely ground black pepper

1 teaspoon dried thyme

½ teaspoon kosher salt

1 teaspoon granulated garlic

2 (1-pound) pork tenderloins, trimmed of excess fat and silverskin (see page 60)

2 tablespoons Dijon mustard

Oil, for the grill

Hoecakes

2 cups self-rising white cornmeal

¾ cup self-rising flour

½ cup finely diced yellow onion

¼ cup finely diced pickled jalapeños

1½ teaspoons kosher salt

2 large eggs, lightly beaten

2 cups buttermilk

2 tablespoons canola oil, or as needed

Pork tenderloin is one of the most versatile cuts of meat available. It serves as a wonderful palette for any number of flavors, from Mexican to Asian and all the places in between. This version has the snap of cracked black pepper set against a jalapeño hoecake and cooling Mississippi caviar. Hoecakes are basically cornbread pancakes. They get their name from field workers who would cook them on the flat metal of the hoe over a fire. They're a wonderful quick bread you can make while grilling your entrée. In fact, if you prepare the caviar in advance and heat your griddle while the tenderloin is grilling, you can cook the hoecakes while the meat rests and serve dinner in 20 minutes.

(continued)

To make the caviar, place all the ingredients in a small mixing bowl, mix well, and refrigerate for at least 2 hours and up to overnight before serving.

To make the pork, prepare a grill to medium heat. Place the pepper, thyme, salt, and granulated garlic in a small bowl and mix well. Cut each tenderloin in half crosswise, massage them with the mustard, then lightly sprinkle with the seasoning mix. Lightly oil the grill grates, then place the tenderloin on the grates and cook for 12 to 15 minutes, turning every 2 minutes or so, until the internal temperature is 140°F. Remove the pork from the grill, cover with aluminum foil, and rest for 5 to 7 minutes.

To make the hoecakes, stir together the cornmeal, flour, onion, jalapeños, salt, eggs, and buttermilk in a medium mixing bowl. Place a griddle on the grill, add the canola oil, and heat. Once the oil is hot, use a large spoon to drop about ¼ cup of the batter on the griddle, and allow the batter to form a pancake shape. Cook for 2 to 3 minutes, flip, and cook for another 2 minutes, or until golden and cooked through. (The hoecakes will absorb the oil, so you may need to add more oil to the griddle after each one.) Repeat with the remaining batter until you have at least 8 hoecakes.

To serve, place 2 hoecakes on each plate. Slice the tenderloin approximately ½ inch thick on a bias and arrange in a shingle pattern across the hoecakes. Top each portion with a large spoonful of the caviar.

Silverskin is a tough membrane on the surface of tenderloins and loins of most meats (pork, lamb, beef, etc.). Use a very sharp filleting knife to remove it to allow for better texture and to let the flavors get further into your meats.

SICILIAN BBQ PIZZA

SERVES 3 TO 4

Dough

- 3½ cups bread flour
- 1 teaspoon instant yeast
- 1½ cups water, lukewarm (98°F to 105°F)
- 1 tablespoon kosher salt
- 2 tablespoons butter, melted, for the pan
- Olive oil, for the pan

Toppings

- ½ cup pizza sauce or plain tomato sauce
- ½ cup Classic BBQ Sauce (page 36), plus more for drizzling
- 8 ounces low-moisture shredded mozzarella
- 8 ounces Pulled Pork (page 50)
- ½ cup thinly sliced red bell pepper
- ½ small red onion, thinly sliced
- ¼ cup candied or pickled jalapeños, for serving
- Handful torn basil leaves, for serving

I might get some hate from my Italian friends for this recipe, but who doesn't love BBQ pizza? And putting all the BBQ pizza toppings on top of a focaccia-style base? Sign me up! Sicilian pizza has a thick rectangular crust, so I adapted my focaccia recipe for it, which works well. You will need a 13 by 18-inch sheet pan (half sheet pan) for this recipe. Prepare the dough a day in advance.

The day before serving, to prepare the dough, whisk together all the ingredients except the butter and olive oil in a large bowl. There should be no pockets of dry flour. Cover with plastic wrap and let rest for 30 minutes, then stretch and fold: Pick up one side of the dough and stretch until there's resistance, then fold it over to the opposite side. Rotate and repeat this step until all four sides have been folded. Cover for 30 minutes, then repeat the stretch and fold again. Cover and let the dough rest anywhere from 8 to 72 hours.

Grease a half sheet pan very well with the butter and a drizzle of olive oil. Place the dough on the pan and stretch it out as far as you can. Drizzle the top of the dough with olive oil, cover, and let sit for 45 minutes.

While the dough is resting, mix the sauces together in a small bowl.

Place the oven rack on the lower third of the oven, and preheat to 500°F. Stretch the dough back out to fill the entire pan. Oil your hands and press into the dough to make little dimples. Spoon the sauce over the dough, and top with the mozzarella, then the pulled pork, bell pepper, and onion. Bake for 20 to 25 minutes, until the pizza is golden and bubbly. Remove from the oven and let cool slightly. Cut and serve with a drizzle of sauce, the jalapeños, and the basil.

SMOKE-BRAISED PORK CHEEKS WITH CALABRIAN COLLARD GREENS AND SALSA VERDE

SERVES 4

Pork Cheeks

3 pounds pork cheeks

2 to 3 tablespoons SPG+ Seasoning (page 45)

2 tablespoons olive oil

1 leek, white and light green parts only, chopped

½ medium sweet onion, diced

¼ cup diced celery

4 cloves garlic, finely minced

⅓ cup dry vermouth

1½ cups white wine

2 cups chicken stock

4 sprigs thyme

1 sprig rosemary

Salsa Verde

Makes ¼ cup

1 bunch parsley, woody stems removed

2 to 3 tablespoons fresh oregano leaves

3 to 4 cloves garlic, peeled

1 lemon, finely zested and juiced

Kosher salt and freshly ground black pepper

2 to 3 ice cubes

2 to 3 anchovy fillets (optional)

½ slice white bread

Calabrian Collard Greens

¼ cup olive oil or bacon grease

½ sweet onion, diced

2 cloves garlic, finely minced

2 tablespoons chopped Calabrian chilies

2½ cups chicken stock

8 cups chopped fresh collard greens

Pinch of sugar

3 tablespoons apple cider vinegar

Kosher salt and freshly ground black pepper

¾ cup grated Parmesan, plus more for serving

Smoke-braising is one of my favorite cooking methods. I love enhancing a braised dish by imbuing it with the flavor of smoke, and these pork cheeks take on that smoke flavor very well. For this recipe, I was inspired by my time in Calabria (the toe of the boot of Italy), where the weather is warm but the people are warmer. I now find myself putting Calabrian chilies in many of the dishes I make at home, including collard greens. (Please don't take my Southern card away!)

This is a faux pas, but I like adding extra herbs to my Italian salsa verde. Traditionally, this salsa verde is made with just Italian parsley, but when I'm making

a Bolognese I'll add rosemary, and for a summery dish I'll add basil. Here, I'm adding just a little fresh oregano—not enough to overpower but just enough to add depth. You can use whatever fresh herb(s) you'd like. You might be confused by the white bread and ice the recipe calls for. The white bread adds a hint of creaminess without adding any additional liquid, and the ice helps shock the parsley so that it stays green.

To make the pork cheeks, preheat a smoker to 250°F. Sprinkle the pork cheeks with the seasoning on all sides and smoke for 30 minutes to 1 hour, or until the internal temperature is 140°F. Remove from the grill and let rest.

In a Dutch oven or heavy-bottomed saucepan, heat the olive oil over medium heat. Add the leek, onion, and celery and cook until the onions are translucent, 4 to 5 minutes. Add the garlic and cook for 30 seconds, being careful not to overcook. Deglaze the pan with the vermouth and let it cook down, then add the wine and cook until the wine reduces by half, about 1 minute. Add the chicken stock, thyme, rosemary, and pork cheeks, and let the mixture simmer, covered, for 1 to 2 hours, or until the pork cheeks are tender.

To make the salsa verde, place all the ingredients in a blender or food processor and process to your desired consistency. Taste and adjust the seasoning as needed.

To make the collard greens, heat the olive oil in a large saucepan over medium heat. Sauté the onions until translucent, 3 to 4 minutes, then add the garlic and cook for about 30 seconds. Stir in the chilies, then add the chicken stock. Add the collard greens and let them cook down for 30 minutes to 1 hour. Add the sugar and vinegar and season with salt and pepper to taste. Before plating, fold in the Parmesan and mix to combine. Then grate fresh Parmesan over the collards.

Plate the pork cheeks on top of the collards, and top the dish with salsa verde.

LOW AND SLOW CRISPY PORK BELLY WITH APPLE PIE MOONSHINE BBQ SAUCE

SERVES 4 TO 6

Pork Belly

½ piece (4 to 5 pounds) skin-on pork belly

½ tablespoon plus 1 teaspoon extra-virgin olive oil, divided

2 to 3 tablespoons Classic BBQ Rub (page 38)

1 teaspoon kosher salt

Apple Pie Moonshine BBQ Sauce

Makes 2 cups

1 teaspoon olive oil

½ medium yellow onion, finely diced

2 teaspoons minced garlic

1 cup apple pie moonshine

1½ cups ketchup

¼ cup Worcestershire sauce

¼ cup honey

1 tablespoon apple pie spice

¼ cup apple cider vinegar

2 tablespoons Classic BBQ Rub (page 38)

I love pork bellies. But of all the pork bellies I've eaten, my favorite bites of low and slow–smoked pork belly are those still attached to a whole hog. Competitive BBQ teams know that the few bites of the lean streaks in the belly, slowly smoked for 18 to 24 hours, are among the best bites on the entire hog.

While cooking a whole hog just for a few bites of pork belly is a bit extreme, this recipe mimics that process by cooking and rendering the belly for 8 hours, then blasting it in a broiler to get crispy skin (something we can't do with a whole hog). This is a straightforward recipe to execute, even though it takes a lot of time to cook. An entire piece of pork belly averages 9 to 11 pounds and is a significant piece for most people to be able to cook. This recipe calls for a half piece, about 4 to 5 pounds, which you can get at many grocery stores or meat markets.

To prepare the pork belly, place a wire rack over a sheet pan. Using paper towels, pat the meat side of the belly dry, then slather it with ½ tablespoon of the olive oil and season the meat thoroughly with the rub. Turn the piece of belly skin side up. Pat it dry, then place the belly in the fridge, uncovered, overnight.

(continued)

PRAIRIE
FRESH

Remove the belly from the fridge and prepare a smoker to cook at 230°F. Lightly oil the skin side of the belly with the remaining 1 teaspoon of the olive oil, then sprinkle with the salt. Place the pork belly in the smoker, skin side up. Cook for 3 hours, then remove the belly and wrap the meat in an aluminum foil "boat," covering up the exposed meat and sides of the belly but not the skin on top. Place on a sheet pan, return to the smoker, and cook for 4 hours.

While the belly is cooking, make the BBQ sauce. Place the olive oil and onion in a small saucepan over medium-high heat. Cook for 2 minutes, then add the garlic and cook for 2 to 3 minutes, until the onions are starting to turn translucent. Add the moonshine, increase the heat to high, and cook for 4 to 5 minutes, or until the liquid is reduced by half. Decrease the heat to medium, add the remaining ingredients, and whisk until thoroughly incorporated. Simmer for 10 minutes.

Leaving the foil on the belly, carefully drain the fats from the foil. Preheat the oven to 450°F. Spread the pork belly as evenly as possible on a sheet pan and cook for 25 to 30 minutes, allowing the skin to crisp up like cracklings. (This method will yield a very tender pork belly beneath the crispy skin.) Cut into portions and serve with the sauce.

BRINED PORK CHOPS WITH BLACKBERRY-SERRANO HONEY MUSTARD

SERVES 4

Brine

- 2 cups water
- ⅓ cup kosher salt
- ¼ cup sugar
- 1 lemon, halved
- 1 medium yellow onion, quartered
- 3 to 4 cloves garlic, peeled and smashed
- 1 tablespoon black peppercorns
- 1 sprig rosemary
- 2 to 3 sprigs sage
- 2 bay leaves
- 3 cups ice

Pork Chops

- 4 (1½ to 2-inch) thick pork chops
- ¼ cup kosher salt
- 2 tablespoons light brown sugar
- 2 tablespoons smoked paprika
- 1 tablespoon granulated garlic
- 1 tablespoon black pepper
- 2 teaspoons dried sage
- ½ teaspoon cayenne pepper
- ½ tablespoon extra-virgin olive oil

Blackberry-Serrano Honey Mustard

Makes 2½ cups

- 6 ounces fresh blackberries
- ⅓ cup sugar
- 2 tablespoons Champagne Mustard (page 47) or stone-ground mustard
- 2 tablespoons yellow mustard
- 2 tablespoons Dijon mustard
- 2 cups mayonnaise
- 1 serrano, seeded and diced
- 1 teaspoon smoked paprika
- 1 teaspoon kosher salt

Pork chops are a great value at the grocery store and have more flavor than chicken breasts. For the best value, buy a half or a whole pork loin and cut it into chops and roasts. I prefer to buy whole pork loins (shoutout to Prairie Fresh pork!), as you can get so many cuts from it. This recipe is for four 1½ to 2-inch-thick pork chops.

The sauce's brilliant purple hue and fresh blackberry flavor make it a striking color pop on anything you serve it with. It works amazingly well with pork or chicken.

(continued)

To make the brine, place the water, salt, and sugar in a large saucepan. Bring to a boil while whisking to ensure the salt and sugar dissolve. Pour the mixture into a nonreactive container and add the lemon, onion, garlic, peppercorns, rosemary, sage, and bay leaves. Let steep for 10 minutes, then stir in the ice.

Place the pork chops in the brine and refrigerate for 3 to 4 hours or up to overnight.

To make the honey mustard, place the blackberries and sugar in a small saucepan and bring to a boil. Use a wooden spoon to stir occasionally and mash the berries as they soften and cook. Decrease the heat to a simmer and continue to cook for 3 to 4 minutes, or until the mixture reduces slightly. Pour the mixture through a fine mesh strainer into a mixing bowl, pressing the berries with the spoon to release any juices. Discard the solids and allow the syrup to cool.

Whisk the remaining blackberry-serrano honey mustard ingredients into the syrup. Store in the fridge until ready to serve. The honey mustard will keep in the fridge for up to 1 week.

To cook the pork chops, prepare a grill with a two-zone fire, using one chimney of charcoal and 2 to 3 chunks of wood placed in half the grill. Remove the pork chops from the brine and pat dry with paper towels. Discard the brine. Place all the pork chops ingredients except the olive oil in a bowl and stir to combine. Slather each side of the pork chops with olive oil, then season both sides with the spice blend. Let the pork come to room temperature, 15 to 20 minutes, before cooking.

Place the chops on the hot side of the grill and cook for 2 minutes, then turn the chops 90 degrees and grill for another 2 minutes. Flip the chops over and repeat. Move the chops to the cool zone of the grill and continue to cook until the internal temperature registers 140°F in the thickest part. Remove from the grill, cover with a piece of aluminum foil, and let rest for 10 minutes.

Smear a generous amount of the honey mustard on a plate, then place the pork chops on top. Serve with additional honey mustard.

PORK TENDERLOIN SOUVLAKI WITH TZATZIKI SAUCE

SERVES 4

- 2 pork tenderloins, silverskin removed
- Kosher salt and coarsely ground black pepper
- ¼ cup red wine
- 3 tablespoons lemon juice
- 2 tablespoons minced garlic
- 2 tablespoons olive oil
- 1 tablespoon paprika
- 1 teaspoon cumin
- 2 tablespoons chopped fresh oregano leaves, divided
- Kosher salt and freshly ground black pepper
- 1 medium yellow onion, cut into wedges

Tzatziki Sauce

Makes about 1½ cups

- 1 cup whole milk Greek yogurt
- ½ cup cucumber, seeded and finely diced or grated
- 1 teaspoon minced garlic
- ½ tablespoon olive oil
- 1 tablespoon chopped fresh dill
- Kosher salt and coarsely ground black pepper

- 4 to 5 pieces pita bread, for serving
- Sprouts, for serving
- Tomato slices, for serving

I like cooking food on skewers. There, I said it. And I mean it. It's fun; the skewered food cooks quickly, and using small pieces of meat increases the surface area and exposes it to more flavor. Souvlaki is of Greek origin and can be made using chicken or pork. While it's usually eaten right off the skewers, I prefer to pull the meat and onions from the skewers and put them on a large platter for serving. Tzatziki sauce is a cool cucumber-and-yogurt sauce perfect for this souvlaki and other Greek dishes or as a dip for veggies or pita chips. If you use wooden skewers, soak them in water for 30 minutes to 1 hour before threading the tenderloin and onions and grilling them.

Cut the tenderloins into ¾-inch pieces and season with salt and pepper. Let sit for 5 minutes.

Whisk together the wine, lemon juice, garlic, olive oil, paprika, cumin, oregano, and salt and pepper in a small bowl. Place the pork and onion in a resealable plastic bag, add the marinade, and press out any air. Refrigerate for at least 2 hours (more time is better), rotating every hour.

While the meat is marinating, make the tzatziki sauce. Combine all the ingredients in a medium bowl and refrigerate until ready to serve. Will keep for 3 to 4 days in the fridge.

Preheat a grill to medium heat. Remove the pork and onions from the marinade and skewer. (I like to put the meat and vegetables on separate skewers.) Discard the marinade. Place the skewers on the grill and cook for 8 to 10 minutes, turning every few minutes. Cook until the internal temperature of the pork registers 140°F, and grill the onion skewers until charred. Remove from the grill and let rest for 5 minutes. Grill the pita bread until warm.

Place the souvlaki and onion skewers on a platter and serve with pita bread, sprouts, tomato slices, and tzatziki sauce.

SPICY SAGE COUNTRY SAUSAGE AND SAUSAGE GRAVY

SERVES 4

Spicy Sage Country Sausage

1 deboned pork butt, about 5 to 7 pounds of meat, cut into small strips, or 80/20 ground pork

2 pounds pork belly, cut into small strips (if using pork butt)

3 tablespoons light brown sugar

2 tablespoons finely chopped fresh sage

2 tablespoons granulated garlic

1½ tablespoons kosher salt

1 tablespoon finely chopped fresh thyme leaves

1 tablespoon black pepper

2 teaspoons smoked paprika

2 teaspoons cayenne pepper or crushed red pepper (optional)

Sausage Gravy

Makes 2½ cups

½ pound cooked sausage patties, crumbled

2 tablespoons all-purpose flour

2 cups milk

1 teaspoon kosher salt

1 teaspoon black pepper

Buttermilk Biscuits (page 29), for serving

The thing about making your own country sausage is that you can adjust it to your taste. An average pork butt has around an 80/20 meat-to-fat ratio. Most pork sausage is better with a 70/30 ratio, so I add a couple of pounds of pork belly to the mix. If you have access to backfat, just use 1 pound.

I usually grab a pork butt, debone it, and cut it into small strips. With the average-size butt, I'll end up with 7 to 8 pounds of sausage, with 1 pound ready to cook and 7 pounds for the freezer. Vacuum-sealed and frozen, the sausage will keep for up to 6 months.

A grinder attachment on your mixer is fine for making uncased sausage. If you want to make cased sausages, look into a sausage stuffer as the little sausage-stuffing funnels for home grinders are not fun to work with and generally yield poor results.

To make the sausage, place the pork butt and the pork belly in a large mixing bowl. Place the remaining ingredients in a small bowl and stir to combine. Sprinkle the seasoning blend over the pork and toss to coat the pieces. Place the pork in the freezer for 20 minutes. (If using ground pork, mix it thoroughly with the seasoning blend and skip the freezer step.)

Using a grinder or an attachment for your mixer, grind the pork through a large plate, then return it the freezer for 20 minutes. Then, using the smaller plate, run the mixture through the grinder again. Pan-fry a small portion of the sausage for tasting and adjust the seasoning as needed.

Cover the pork and refrigerate overnight. To make sausage patties, mix the pork with your hands and use 1½ pounds to form 3-inch patties.

Portion the remaining sausage mixture into 1-pound increments for later use. For best results, vacuum-seal each pound of sausage, then label, date, and freeze for up to 6 months.

To make the gravy, line a plate with a paper towel. In a heavy-bottomed skillet over medium-high heat, cook the sausage patties until they are browned and the internal temperature registers at least 165°F, 3 to 4 minutes per side. Set on the plate to drain.

Lower the heat to medium. Whisk the flour into the rendered drippings and cook until a blond roux is formed and the flour is cooked, 5 to 7 minutes. Add the milk in ½ cup increments, whisking thoroughly to incorporate and waiting until the gravy returns to a simmer and thickens. Cook until the desired viscosity is reached. Add the crumbled sausage and stir. Add the salt and pepper; taste and adjust the seasoning as needed.

To serve, open the buttermilk biscuits in half and top them with the gravy. Serve with sausages, eggs, and other breakfast favorites.

CRISPY ALSATIAN PORK KNUCKLES

SERVES 4

Pork Knuckles

- 2 large pork knuckles from the ham, about 2 pounds each
- ½ cup white vinegar, divided
- ½ tablespoon kosher salt
- 1 teaspoon coarsely ground black pepper
- 1 teaspoon caraway seeds
- 1 teaspoon juniper berries
- ½ teaspoon fennel seeds
- 1 teaspoon yellow mustard seeds
- ½ teaspoon cloves

Gravy

Makes 2 cups

- 2 cups chicken stock
- 12 ounces dark beer
- ½ cup chopped carrot
- 1 medium yellow onion, coarsely chopped
- 3 bay leaves
- 3 to 4 cloves garlic
- 1 tablespoon apple cider vinegar
- 1 tablespoon Champagne Mustard (page 47)
- 1 teaspoon sugar
- Kosher salt and finely ground black pepper
- 2 tablespoons cornstarch
- ½ cup water

Alsace is a small region in France situated next to Germany. Alsatians have a lot of German influences in their food but manage to keep it uniquely French. This includes their way of cooking sauerkraut (*choucroute* in French). While visiting the region, I dined on a delicious braised pork knuckle served with sauerkraut. This is my version with a twist, as there is not much of a culture of smoking food there. While the meat I ate was delicious, this version blasts the skin to create a flavorful crackling.

When I was competing in BBQ contests with whole shoulders, my favorite bites were out of the shank. The meat, cooked in the middle of the fat and skin of the collar, was terrific. It had a different texture from the rest of the shoulder, and I would only give some of it to very experienced judges who could appreciate the various textures and flavors.

For this recipe, ask your butcher to order you ham knuckles as they are larger and will have better meat and skin. Instead of putting them on a roasting pan and rack, I prefer to set the pork knuckles on a wire rack placed over a half-size aluminum pan. This keeps the skin out of the gravy and allows the drippings and smoky flavor to infuse the gravy while keeping the meat moist.

Serve this with a dry Riesling and enjoy!

To make the pork knuckles, dry the skin on the knuckles and use a knife to lightly score or prick them all over. (Be careful not to prick all the way to the meat so the meat does not dry out.) Stretch the skin out and run two metal skewers through the knuckles, near the large end of the shank.

(continued)

Brush the skin and meat with half of the vinegar. In a small bowl, mix together the remaining pork knuckles ingredients Thoroughly season the exposed meat, then rub the remaining seasoning over the skin. Refrigerate the knuckles, standing up, overnight to dry-brine and dry the skin.

Prepare an indirect smoker to cook at 350°F. Use only 1 to 2 chunks of applewood for a light smoke flavor and to prevent the knuckle skin from turning too dark.

To make the gravy, place all the ingredients except the cornstarch and water in a half sheet pan, place a wire rack over it, and set the knuckles on top. Stick a meat thermometer into the meatiest part of a knuckle and cook until the internal temperature reaches 190°F to 200°F, about 2½ hours. Remove the pan from the smoker and let the knuckles rest for 15 minutes. Brush the skin of the knuckles with vinegar again.

Preheat the oven to 500°F (with convection heat if you have it). Put the knuckles on a sheet pan and roast for 30 minutes to bubble the skin. Remove them from the oven and let rest for 10 to 15 minutes while you finish the gravy.

In a small bowl, whisk together the cornstarch and water to create a slurry. Pour the stock and vegetables through a fine mesh strainer into a medium saucepan, pressing the vegetables to release any juices. Discard the vegetables. Whisk the cornstarch slurry into the liquid and bring to a boil. Remove from the heat when thickened, then whisk and pour into a gravy boat.

To serve, drizzle the gravy over the whole knuckles.

5

BEEF/LAMB/GOAT

RIB EYE "OLD FASHIONED" WITH SMOKED PEPPERCORNS AND CHERRY BOURBON SAUCE

SERVES 2

Cherry Bourbon Sauce

Makes 2 cups

- **8 ounces cherries (fresh preferred), pitted**
- **1 tablespoon unsalted butter**
- **1 shallot, minced**
- **⅓ cup bourbon**
- **2 sprigs thyme tied with 1 sprig rosemary**
- **1 teaspoon bitters**
- **½ teaspoon kosher salt**
- **½ teaspoon black pepper**
- **½ cup beef stock**
- **2 to 3 tablespoons heavy cream**

Rib Eye

- **2 (12-ounce) rib eye steaks, about 1 inch thick**
- **½ tablespoon olive oil**
- **1 tablespoons Melissa Cookston Grillin' Shake or SPG+ Seasoning (page 45)**
- **3 tablespoons Bourbon-Infused Smoked Peppercorns (page 79) or regular peppercorns, cracked in a mortar and pestle**

For this recipe's inspiration, I just went with the classic bourbon cocktail, the old fashioned. I've always been a rib eye girl, and this one checks a lot of boxes for me: delicious grilled rib eye, lots of pepper, and a tasty unique sauce. The smoked cherries may be prepared ahead of time, then frozen or dehydrated thoroughly to keep for 3 to 4 months in an airtight container. If you're using dehydrated smoked cherries, soak them in the bourbon for 30 minutes before making the sauce.

To make the sauce, prepare a smoker to cook at 200°F to 225°F with cherrywood. Place the cherries in a small metal pan, then place in the smoker for 2 hours. Remove the pan from the smoker and let cool.

Place the butter in a small saucepan over medium-high heat. Add the shallot and cook for 2 to 3 minutes, or until the shallots are softened. Increase the heat to high, add the bourbon, thyme and rosemary, bitters, and cherries, and boil until almost fully reduced, 2 to 3 minutes. Decrease the heat to medium and add the salt, pepper, and beef stock. Bring to a boil, then decrease to a simmer. Whisk in the cream, taste and adjust the seasoning as needed, and simmer until the desired thickness is reached. Keep warm over very low heat until ready to serve.

To make the steaks, pat the steaks dry with paper towels, then rub both sides with the olive oil and shake. Place the cracked peppercorns on a plate and press the steaks on them to crust one side.

Preheat a grill to medium-high heat, about 450°F. Place the steaks on the hot part of the grill, peppered side up, and grill for 2 minutes, then rotate 90 degrees and cook for another 2 minutes. Carefully turn the steaks over and repeat the cooking process. This should yield a medium-rare rib eye, but test with a meat thermometer. Continue to cook until your desired temperature is reached, then place the steaks on a platter, peppered side up. Lightly cover and rest for 5 to 10 minutes. Serve with the Cherry Bourbon Sauce.

BOURBON-INFUSED SMOKED PEPPERCORNS

½ cup black peppercorns

3 ounces bourbon

Bourbon-infused smoked peppercorns are a tasty option for steak au poivre.

Place the peppercorns and bourbon in a pint jar. Put the lid on the jar and set on the counter for 2 to 3 days. Then empty the jar into a small aluminum pan and preheat the smoker to cook at 225°F with hickory. Smoke for 2 to 3 hours, or until all the whiskey has evaporated. Cool the peppercorns, place them back in the jar, and cover with the lid. When ready to use, pour out the desired amount and crack the peppercorns with a mortar and pestle.

BRISKET AND BURNT ENDS

MAKES 4 TO 5 POUNDS

House Brisket Rub

- 1 cup kosher salt
- ½ cup granulated garlic
- ¼ cup coarsely ground black pepper

Brisket

- 1 (10 to 12-pound) choice-grade whole beef brisket
- 2½ tablespoons yellow mustard, divided

Burnt Ends

- 2 tablespoons Classic BBQ Rub (page 38)
- 1 cup Classic BBQ Sauce (page 36)

There is a definite difference in my barbecue depending on whether I'm cooking at a contest or for family and friends. When cooking for myself and my family, I am not as worried about one-bite flavor or pleasing the majority of the judges' palates. When cooking at home, I can cook what my family and I love. This is a simple old-school brisket, complete with a rich, deep crust and a dense smoke flavor. And while I have turned in similar briskets that have done well in competition, cooking this recipe is about expressing a more traditional flavor than most judges expect. The brisket and burnt ends will keep in resealable plastic bags in the freezer for up to 2 months. You will also have leftover rub, and it will keep in an airtight container for about 1 month.

Prepare a smoker to cook at 250°F. I prefer pecan wood, but any milder wood will do. I use 4 to 6 chunks of wood through the first 3 hours, then replenish it, but I don't use any more wood after I wrap the meat in foil.

To make the rub, mix all the ingredients together in a small bowl.

To make the brisket, remove any fat pockets from the surface of the flat part of the brisket and any surface fat from the top of the point. Sprinkle the meat side with 2 tablespoons of the rub, then top with 1½ tablespoons of the mustard and massage it into the meat. Place the brisket in the smoker, meat side up, and cook for 6 hours or until the internal temperature registers 150°F to 160°F.

(continued)

Remove the brisket and place it in a large aluminum pan. Season with 1 tablespoon of the rub and the remaining 1 tablespoon of mustard, and massage them into the meat. Return the pan to the smoker and cook until the internal temperature reaches 202°F or a meat probe slides in easily, 3 to 4 more hours. Remove the pan from the smoker and let the brisket cool for 5 minutes.

Pour off the drippings into another container and set aside. Using a sharp boning knife and wearing heatproof gloves, slice through the fat between the point and the flat to separate the pieces. Leave the flat of the brisket in the pan, cover, and place in an empty cooler or insulated Cambro for 1 to 2 hours to rest.

To make the burnt ends, place the point of the brisket on a cutting board and remove the exterior fat. Slice horizontally through the middle of the point, then cut into 1-inch-square pieces. Place the pieces in a small pan, season with the rub, and pour in the sauce and ½ cup of the beef drippings. Stir to coat the pieces. Place the pan, uncovered, in the smoker for 1½ hours, or until the sauce is caramelized around the ends.

To serve, remove the flat from the pan, reserving any accumulated drippings. Cut into ¼-inch slices across the grain and serve with the burnt ends and the drippings.

SALANTOURMASI (GREEK STUFFED ONIONS)

SERVES 4 TO 6

Salantourmasi

4 to 6 large yellow onions

Filling

3 tablespoons olive oil

1 medium yellow onion, diced

6 cloves garlic, minced

1 pound ground beef

1 pound ground lamb

Kosher salt and freshly ground black pepper

2 tablespoons finely chopped shelled pistachios

1 cup puréed tomatoes (canned is fine)

1 cup Arborio rice

1½ cups chicken stock

2 teaspoons chopped fresh oregano leaves, plus more for garnish

2 teaspoons chopped fresh mint leaves, plus more for garnish

2 teaspoons chopped fresh dill, plus more for garnish

2 tablespoons chopped Italian parsley leaves, plus more for garnish

Sauce

2 cups puréed tomatoes (canned is fine)

2 cups chicken stock

2 tablespoons balsamic vinegar

Kosher salt and finely ground black pepper

I've decided that onions (or any member of the allium family, for that matter) are among my most favorite ingredients. Adding them to some of my other favorite ingredients, like beef, lamb, and herbs, to create an absolute flavor bomb just makes sense! I love making stuffed onions in the fall and winter, and they're great with a green salad and yogurt.

(continued)

To make the salantourmasi, peel the onions and cut the tops and bottoms off each one. Make a light slit down a side of each onion, but do not cut through the layers.

Bring a pot of salted water to a boil. Boil the onions for 10 to 12 minutes, until softened. Drain and let cool. Gently separate the layers, making sure to keep the onions intact for stuffing.

To make the filling, heat the olive oil in a skillet over medium heat. Add the diced onion and cook until softened, 5 to 6 minutes. Add the garlic and cook until fragrant, about 1 minute. Add the ground beef and lamb and cook until no longer pink. Season with salt and pepper and add the pistachios.

Add the puréed tomatoes and cook until slightly thickened. Add the rice and chicken stock and cook until the rice absorbs the stock, 7 to 8 minutes. Remove from the heat and stir in the herbs.

Preheat the oven or grill to 375°F. Place a spoonful of the filling in the center of an onion layer. Fold the layer around the filling to create a little pocket. Repeat with the remaining filling and onion layers. Arrange the onions in an aluminum pan, seam side down and close together, so they do not unroll while cooking.

To make the sauce, mix all the ingredients together in a bowl. Pour over the onions, cover the pan, and bake for 45 minutes. Uncover the pan and continue to bake until brown and caramelized, 30 to 40 minutes. Garnish with the herbs and serve.

SMOKED MEATLOAF WITH CHARRED TOMATO GRAVY

SERVES 2 TO 4

Charred Tomato Gravy

Makes about 1½ cups

- 6 Roma tomatoes, halved
- 2 Anaheim or Hatch chiles
- ½ tablespoon Smoke-Roasted Garlic (page 46)
- 1 tablespoon olive oil
- 3 thick bacon slices
- 2 tablespoons all-purpose flour
- 1 cup chicken stock
- ½ teaspoon kosher salt
- ¼ teaspoon finely ground black pepper
- 1 tablespoon brown sugar (optional)
- 1½ teaspoons smoked paprika

Smoked Meatloaf

- 1 medium onion, diced
- 1 medium green bell pepper, diced
- 1 tablespoon canola or neutral oil
- 1 tablespoon minced garlic
- 2 pounds 80/20 ground beef
- ¼ cup Classic BBQ Sauce (page 36)
- ¼ cup Classic BBQ Rub (page 38), plus more for sprinkling
- ¾ cup Charred Tomato Gravy, plus more for glazing and serving
- 2 eggs, lightly whisked
- ⅓ cup panko breadcrumbs
- 1½ tablespoons Melissa Cookston Woo Woo Sauce or 2½ tablespoons Worcestershire sauce
- 1 teaspoon kosher salt
- ½ teaspoon finely ground black pepper

Meatloaf is one of the all-time classic comfort dishes. It's super easy to cook in the smoker to imbue it with some smoky flavor.

Tomato gravy is a Southern sauce served with everything from eggs to pizza, on crusty garlic bread, or even as a delicious pasta sauce. I'm using this version to top my smoked meatloaf, so I added roasted Hatch peppers and charred the tomatoes before mixing in the gravy to add more flavor to the sauce. Make the gravy beforehand so you can use some in the meatloaf, then generously serve over each slice.

To make the gravy, lightly grease a sheet pan and preheat the oven to 400°F. Place the tomato halves, cut side down, chiles, and garlic on the pan. Toss with the olive oil and roast for 40 minutes, or until the tomatoes are lightly charred. Remove the pan from the oven and place the chiles in a paper bag or resealable plastic bag and close. Let cool in the bag, then peel off the skin and stem, seed, and finely chop.

Line a plate with a paper towel. In a heavy-bottomed large skillet or saucepan, fry the bacon until crisp. Set on the plate to cool.

Whisk the flour into the bacon fat and cook over medium-low heat for 10 to 15 minutes, until a roux forms. Whisk in the chicken stock in small amounts until a gravy forms. Add the tomatoes and garlic, including any juices in the pan. Add the chiles, salt, pepper, brown sugar (if using), and paprika. Break the bacon into small pieces and add to the gravy. Bring the gravy to a simmer and stir, breaking up the tomato pieces with a spoon. Cook for 10 to 15 minutes. Taste and adjust the seasoning as needed, then remove from the heat.

To make the meatloaf, preheat the smoker to cook at 350°F. In a small skillet, sauté the onion and bell pepper in the canola oil for 4 to 5 minutes, or until softened. Add the garlic and cook for another 2 to 3 minutes, or until golden and fragrant. Remove from the heat and let cool.

In a large bowl, lightly mix together the ground beef, onion mixture, sauce, rub, tomato gravy, eggs, panko, Woo Woo Sauce, salt, and pepper.

Lightly grease a 9 by 5-inch casserole pan with the canola oil. Press the meatloaf mixture firmly into the pan, leaving a 1-inch space on one end. Place the pan in the smoker and cook until the internal temperature reaches 170°F, about 1 hour. Drain the grease, then glaze the meatloaf with the tomato gravy. Cook for 10 minutes, then remove from the smoker and let rest for 10 minutes. Slice and serve with the tomato gravy.

MISO TERIYAKI SHORT RIBS WITH QUICK-PICKLED WATERMELON RADISH

SERVES 4

Marinade

¼ cup miso (white preferred)

1 cup beef stock

½ cup soy sauce

⅓ cup dark brown sugar

1 clove garlic, minced

1 teaspoon minced fresh ginger

1 tablespoon honey

2 teaspoons sesame oil

3 tablespoons mirin

Short Ribs

2 pounds English-cut beef short ribs

½ tablespoon Melissa Cookston Grillin' Shake or SPG+ Seasoning (page 45)

Watermelon Radish

6 to 8 watermelon radishes, peeled and very thinly sliced

¾ cup rice vinegar

¾ cup sugar

¾ cup water

½ teaspoon kosher salt

3 cloves garlic, peeled and smashed

½ teaspoon red pepper flakes

Glaze

1 tablespoon cornstarch

¼ cup cold water

Cooked rice, for serving

1 tablespoon white sesame seeds, for garnish

1 tablespoon chopped green onion, for garnish

I will say it: I love short ribs more than I like brisket. Each bite brings an explosion of unctuous beef goodness to the palate. Short ribs are an excellent dish to braise, and they seem to meld effortlessly with rich, beefy flavors or Asian-influenced flavors. The quick-pickled watermelon radishes help cut the richness of the dish and provide a nice flavor counterpoint.

(continued)

To make the marinade, place all the ingredients in a small saucepan and whisk together over medium heat. Bring to a boil, then decrease the heat and simmer for 3 to 4 minutes. Remove from the heat, let cool, and reserve half the marinade.

Place the short ribs in a resealable bag with the remaining cooled marinade. Refrigerate for at least 4 hours or up to overnight.

To make the watermelon radish, place the radishes in a mason jar and pack them down. In a small saucepan over medium heat, whisk together the remaining ingredients until the sugar fully dissolves. Remove from the heat and let cool. Pour the vinegar mixture into the jar, ensuring the liquid covers the radishes. Place the lid on the jar and let sit for 30 minutes before serving, or store in the fridge for up to 2 weeks.

To finish the short ribs, prepare a smoker to cook at 275°F. Remove the short ribs from the marinade and save the marinade. Using paper towels, pat the short ribs dry, then season them with the shake. Place the short ribs in the smoker and cook for 2 hours. Then place the short ribs in a small aluminum pan, add the marinade they were in, and turn them over a few times to coat. Cover the pan with aluminum foil and cook in the smoker for 2 hours, or until very tender.

While the short ribs are finishing, make the glaze. Place the reserved marinade in a small saucepan. Mix the cornstarch and water, whisk, and add to the marinade. Continue whisking and bring to a boil. Remove from the heat when it reaches a glaze-like consistency.

Remove the pan from the smoker, transfer the short ribs to a plate, brush with the glaze, and serve over rice. Garnish with the sesame seeds, green onions, and watermelon radishes.

BISTECCA ALLA FIORENTINA

SERVES 2

Florentine Grill Seasoning

- 3 tablespoons kosher or sea salt
- 1 tablespoon granulated garlic
- 1 tablespoon coarsely ground black pepper
- ½ teaspoon dried oregano
- ½ teaspoon crushed dried rosemary

Steak

- 1 (3-inch) thick dry-aged porterhouse steak, about 2.5 pounds
- Florentine Grill Seasoning or kosher salt and coarsely ground black pepper
- Firenze Steak Sauce (see Note) (optional)

Bistecca alla Fiorentina is just a marvelously large dry-aged porterhouse steak that is simply grilled. It is a specialty of the Tuscan region of Italy, and especially Florence, one of my favorite cities. As you walk through Florence, you will pass many small restaurants with glass meat cases where you can see their steaks on display.

One of the best steaks I have had was at a local restaurant in Florence. Walking through the town in the afternoon, my husband paused to look in the restaurant's meat case, and an older gentleman (obviously the owner) asked us to come in. He was friendly, and we decided to go to the restaurant that evening. The service was outstanding, and even though the meal was over two hours long, it seemed to go by quickly. We could see our server go into deep thinking mode when discussing wine with us, as he went through the selections to pick the perfect bottle. When we chose the bistecca as our meal, he went through several steaks in the case and discussed each one's weight with us (they charged by the ounce) and his thoughts on how it would cook up for us. I have never had such thoughtfulness go into my meal, and it was greatly appreciated, as the meal could not have been better.

Bistecca alla Fiorentina is traditionally prepared with Chianina beef raised in Italy. Chianina beef is a breed, just as are Angus, Hereford, or Piedmontese. While I have seen it very occasionally for sale online, instead of trying to get Chianina, get a very good–quality thick (think 3 inches thick) dry-aged (most important) porterhouse. For best results, the steak should be dry to the touch before grilling. A good dry-aged steak will be fine; just leave it sitting out for about 30 minutes before grilling. If you cut your steak yourself, you may want to put it on a rack in the fridge for 6 to 8 hours to let the surface dry.

(continued)

This is usually served rare but with a beautiful deep, rich crust owing to the thickness of the steak. If you're cooking to any temperature higher than rare, you'll need to use an oven or an indirect grill, which I think causes it to lose some of the flavor. I prefer to cook this steak on an open wood-fired grill, but you can also cook it on a gas or charcoal grill. Set up the grill for a two-zone fire. If you desire to go above rare to medium rare, follow the instructions and then put the steak on the indirect side of the grill to reach your desired temperature.

After cooking this, you'll definitely want to have a friend with you to share this beautiful steak.

To make the Florentine seasoning, mix all the ingredients together in a small bowl.

To make the steak, sprinkle each side of the steak liberally with the Florentine seasoning. (I've seen many restaurants in Italy simply grill the steak without seasoning, then add some sea salt.)

Oil the grill grates and preheat the grill to 500°F. Place the steak on the grill and cook for 4 to 5 minutes, then give it a quarter turn and cook for another 4 to 5 minutes. Flip the steak and repeat. Set the steak up on the bone and cook for 3 to 4 minutes. Remove from the grill and let rest for 5 to 8 minutes.

Slice the steak from the bone and serve with the sauce, if using, to dredge the flavorful beef.

Firenze Steak Sauce is a bit of a misnomer, as it is simply good olive oil mixed with freshly cracked salt and freshly ground pepper. While simple, it sets off the bistecca so well. Use good olive oil. This "sauce" should not be prepared in advance; rather, the diner should have the option to make it on their plate. Have your guests drizzle about 1 teaspoon of good olive oil on their plate, add two good pinches of salt and pepper, and mix well.

SMOKED OXTAIL PEPOSO WITH GREMOLATA

SERVES 2 TO 4

Gremolata

½ bunch Italian parsley, large stems removed, finely chopped

1 clove garlic, grated

Zest from 1 medium lemon

1 tablespoon chopped fresh basil leaves

½ teaspoon kosher salt

Oxtail

4 to 6 pounds oxtail

1 tablespoon kosher salt

1 tablespoon coarsely ground black pepper

1 tablespoon olive oil

1 medium yellow onion, diced

4 cloves garlic, lightly mashed

1 tablespoon crushed black peppercorns

1 cup beef broth

1 (750-ml) bottle good Chianti

1 (14-ounce) can diced tomatoes

2 tablespoons tomato paste

2 bay leaves

1 bunch fresh thyme, tied together

Noodles, rice, or polenta, for serving

Peposo is a lovely traditional beef and black pepper stew that warms up a cool fall evening. It can be made with beef shank or beef chuck, but I love the gelatinous sensuousness of cooking it with oxtail.

Speaking of tradition, most *peposo* recipes have only five ingredients: beef, garlic, peppercorns, salt, and beef. I haven't made many changes to this recipe, but if you want to be über-traditional, ignore any instructions that don't address these five ingredients.

Gremolata is one of the easiest condiments to make, taking only 4 to 5 minutes. Like chermoula and chimichurri, gremolata is an herbal condiment that, instead of turning into a sauce with the addition of liquids and olive oil, is used as a flavoring sprinkle. It brings fresh citrusy notes to dishes. The deep, rich wine flavor of the *peposo* benefits immensely from the gremolata.

Peposo is not as thick as some other stews, as there is no flour added to thicken the broth. *Peposo* is so rich and flavorful, you won't miss it. This is a straightforward recipe with only a few ingredients, but one is an entire bottle of Chianti. Get a good Chianti for this recipe. "If you wouldn't drink it, don't cook with it" is a good motto when selecting wine for cooking.

To make the gremolata, place the parsley, garlic, lemon zest, basil, and salt in a small bowl and toss with a fork until incorporated. The gremolata will keep in the fridge for up to 3 days, but it's best when it's fresh.

To prepare the oxtail, preheat the smoker to cook at 250°F. Season the oxtail on all sides with the salt and pepper. Place in the smoker and cook for 1½ hours.

Remove the oxtail from the smoker and raise the heat to 275°F. Heat a large pan on the smoker, add the olive oil, onion, and garlic, and cook for 3 to 4 minutes. Add the oxtail and the remaining ingredients and stir to combine. Cover and cook for 3 to 4 hours, until the meat is tender and falling from the bones.

Remove the beef from the bones. Pour the liquid from the pan into a fat separator and let sit until separated. Pour off the grease and discard, then pour the remaining liquid back into the pan and add the beef. Heat until warm, then taste and adjust the seasoning as needed. Serve over noodles, rice, or polenta.

BEEF ANTICUCHOS WITH AJÍ PANCA SAUCE

MAKES 8 SKEWERS

Anticuchos

- 1 pound teres major or other tender cut of beef, cut into ¾-inch cubes
- ½ cup ají panca paste
- ¼ cup olive oil
- 6 cloves garlic, minced
- 1 tablespoon red wine vinegar
- 2 teaspoons dried oregano
- 2 teaspoons ground cumin
- 2 teaspoons smoked paprika
- 1 teaspoon turmeric
- 2 teaspoons sea salt
- 1 teaspoon black pepper

Ají Panca Sauce

Makes 1½ cups

- ½ cup ají panca paste
- ¼ cup soy sauce
- ¼ cup honey
- 1 tablespoon fish sauce
- 1 tablespoon mirin
- 1 tablespoon minced cilantro leaves
- 1 teaspoon Smoke-Roasted Garlic (page 46) or minced garlic
- Zest of ½ lime
- Juice of 1 lime, or 2 tablespoons
- 1 teaspoon sea salt
- ½ teaspoon coarsely ground black pepper

Beef anticuchos are one of the "soul foods" of Peru. This dish is traditionally made with beef heart, which has been marinated, skewered, and grilled. I'm using teres major steaks, which are cut from the chuck section and viewed as the second most tender cut of steak available. Also known as chuck tender, shoulder tender, or petit tender, these steaks aren't usually front and center in the supermarket. It's best to ask your butcher to order them for you, as most of these end up in restaurants with "steak" as one option. Most of the time, butchers handle them poorly, as you need to know how to trim and cut them if you are portioning them as a steak. As anticuchos, however, not much extra knowledge is required—it's a tender cut, and you will cut the meat into small cubes anyway. If you can't find teres major steaks, you can substitute beef tenderloin.

(continued)

To make the anticuchos, mix all the ingredients together in a bowl. Place the beef and marinade in a resealable bag and refrigerate for at least 2 hours. While the beef is marinating, soak 8 small wooden skewers in water.

To prepare the ají panca sauce, combine all the ingredients in a small bowl.

Preheat a grill to 450°F. (The skewers will grill over open flames.) Brush and oil the grates. Remove the meat from the marinade and skewer. Grill the skewers for 3 to 4 minutes, turning often to cook evenly. Brush with the sauce and serve immediately. This dish serves 2 or 3 per person as an entrée with rice and beans or veggies.

CRETAN GOAT AND TOMATO STEW

SERVES 4 TO 6

- **3 pounds cubed bone-in goat meat, preferably from a young goat**
- **3 to 4 tablespoons olive oil**
- **2 medium yellow onions**
- **2 tablespoons Smoke-Roasted Garlic (page 46)**
- **1 tablespoon tomato paste**
- **1 cup red wine**
- **2 to 3 sprigs thyme**
- **1 large sprig rosemary**
- **1 sprig oregano or 1 teaspoon dried oregano**
- **1 (14.5-ounce) can fire-roasted diced tomatoes**
- **1 teaspoon chicken stock base**
- **1 teaspoon honey**
- **1 teaspoon salt**
- **½ teaspoon black pepper**
- **Chopped Italian parsley leaves, for garnish**

A simple wine and olive oil–tasting trip on the Greek island of Crete led to one of my most memorable lunches. We enjoyed learning about Grecian olive oils and tasted some fantastic local wines. With most wine tours, the winery provides some simple snacks or hors d'oeuvres that complement their wines. However, this winery put out a lunch that would favorably compare to many fine dining meals I have had. The wine was fantastic, but the star of the lunch was a traditional Cretan Goat Stew.

In a large Dutch oven, brown the goat meat in the olive oil over medium-high heat. Transfer the goat meat to a plate. Add the onions to the pot and cook for 4 to 5 minutes, until softened. Add the garlic and tomato paste and cook for 1 to 2 minutes. Deglaze the pan with the wine, then add the thyme, rosemary, oregano, tomatoes, chicken stock base, honey, salt, and pepper. Add the goat meat, then bring to a boil. Decrease the heat to a simmer and cover. Simmer for 2 to 2½ hours, or until the goat meat is tender and the sauce has reduced some. Sprinkle with parsley and serve.

BAVETTE STEAK WITH RED WINE–BRAISED DAIKON AND CIPOLLINI ONIONS

SERVES 3 TO 4

Red Wine–Braised Daikon and Cipollini Onions

1 medium daikon

12 ounces cipollini onions

2 tablespoons avocado oil

1 cup beef stock

1 tablespoon soy sauce

1 tablespoon Smoke-Roasted Garlic (page 46)

1 teaspoon gochugaru

1 teaspoon brown sugar

½ tablespoon SPG+ Seasoning (page 45)

1 cup dry red wine

Bavette Steak

1 whole bavette steak, 3 to 4 pounds

½ cup SPG+ Seasoning (page 45)

Fresh chives, for garnish

Bavette steak, also known as flap steak, is cut from the bottom sirloin and has a rich beefy flavor and tenderness. It is known for being served in French bistros and is similar in flavor to flank steak or hanger steak. If time permits, I like to season the steaks with SPG+ Seasoning a few hours before cooking to overnight, then lightly season again before grilling.

Whole flap steaks usually weigh around 4 to 5 pounds untrimmed. If you have an entire bavette, you'll need to trim the exterior fat and silverskin before cooking. You can cut it into smaller steaks, or you can cook a whole steak as a delicious roast. Since the steak is so heavily marbled, a 4 to 6-ounce cut is usually plenty for a serving.

Daikon is a large white radish common in Asian cuisine. I love its mild flavor and peppery pop. It can get bitter as it grows larger, so try to select younger, smaller radishes. Braising daikon in red wine brings out its sweetness and gives hints of pepper—a nice counterpoint for the meal.

To prepare the daikon, using a vegetable peeler, peel the daikon until the veins aren't visible. Cut into ½-inch rounds, then use the peeler to ensure there are no nicks on the sides. Bring a small pot of water to a boil, then trim the root ends off the onions. Boil the onions for 2 to 3 minutes, then place the onions in an ice bath for 3 minutes. Squeeze the onions to remove the skins.

Heat the avocado oil in a skillet over medium-high heat. Sear the daikon for 2 to 3 minutes on each side, or until caramelized. Add the onions and cook for 2 minutes. Add the beef stock, soy sauce, garlic, gochugaru, brown sugar, seasoning, and wine. Cover the pan, decrease the heat to medium-low, and braise for 30 to 45 minutes, or until the radish is fork-tender. As the radish braises, ensure the sauce doesn't thicken too much and add as much water as necessary to keep it from burning.

Transfer the daikon and onions to a plate. Increase the heat and cook the sauce until it is thick and syrupy, 10 to 15 minutes.

Prepare a grill to medium-high heat with a two-zone fire. Sprinkle the steak with the seasoning. Place on the hot side of the grill and cook for 2 minutes, then turn 90 degrees for nice grill marks and cook for another 2 minutes. Flip the steak and repeat. Move to the cooler side of the grill, then bring the steak up to the desired temperature. I like to pull it at 140°F so it's medium-rare. (Flap steaks are thin and can overcook easily, so keep a close eye on your internal meat temperatures.) Remove the steak and let rest for 7 to 10 minutes, then slice into portions.

To serve, pour the sauce on a plate, place the steak over the sauce, serve with the daikon rounds and onions, and garnish with chives.

SMOKY TRI-TIP TORTAS WITH CHIPOTLE CREMOSA

MAKES 6 TO 8 SANDWICHES

Chipotle Cremosa

Makes ½ cup

- 2 chipotles in adobo sauce
- 1 tablespoon Smoke-Roasted Garlic (page 46)
- ¼ cup apple cider vinegar
- ¼ cup water
- 1 tablespoon tomato paste
- 1 teaspoon smoked paprika
- ½ teaspoon onion powder
- ½ teaspoon ground cumin
- Juice of 1 lime
- 1 cup avocado oil

Tri-Tip

- 2 tablespoons SPG+ Seasoning (page 45)
- 1 tablespoon ancho chili powder
- 1 teaspoon brown sugar
- 1 teaspoon ground cumin
- 1 teaspoon Mexican oregano or Mediterranean oregano leaves
- ¼ to ½ teaspoon cayenne pepper (optional)
- 1 (2 to 3-pound) tri-tip
- 2 tablespoons lime juice
- 8 whole jalapeños

Tortas

- 6 to 8 bolillos
- 1 tablespoon granulated garlic
- ½ cup (1 stick) salted butter, melted
- 2 avocados, mashed

Queso fresco, cilantro leaves, pickled red onions, lettuce, mayo, and other condiments, for serving

Tortas are Mexican sandwiches that are full of flavor. Bolillos, a type of oval-shaped bread roll, are perfect for these sandwiches. After toasting, bolillos have a wonderful crusty exterior and soft inside. I love a good piece of tri-tip with a smoky grilled flavor. Flank or skirt steak would also work great for this recipe, though you must adjust cooking times and temperatures.

Cremosa is a variety of salsa that's blended until there aren't any visible chunks. There are numerous variations on this dish. It's perfect to use as a flavorful dip, a taco sauce, or a zippy flavor addition to any dish. Cremosa can be prepared up to 4 days in advance and stored in the fridge. I love the rich sienna color you get from this recipe, and it's wonderful with other peppers. If you use a fresh chipotle, roast it until softened and remove the skin before using.

To make the cremosa, place all the ingredients except the avocado oil in a blender and purée. With the blender running on low speed, drizzle the avocado oil into the mixture. Store in the fridge for up to 5 days.

To make the tri-tip, prepare a grill to medium-hot with a two-zone fire with 2 to 3 wood chunks such as cherry, hickory, or pecan.

Mix together the seasoning, chili powder, brown sugar, cumin, oregano, and cayenne pepper, if using, in a bowl. Dry the steak, then brush with the lime juice. Thoroughly sprinkle the seasoning mix over all sides of the steak.

Place the meat on the cool side of the grill. Cook for 40 to 50 minutes, turning occasionally, until the internal temperature registers 135°F or your desired doneness is reached.

After 20 minutes of cooking, place the jalapeños on the grill. Move to the hot side of the grill and char each side, about a minute per side. Remove the tri-tip from the grill and let rest for 10 to 15 minutes.

To make the tortas, cut the bolillos in half. Mix the granulated garlic with the butter, then butter the cut sides of the bolillos. Toast on the grill for 3 to 5 minutes.

Thinly slice the tri-tip. Spread the avocado on the bottom half of the bolillo, then top with tri-tip and cremosa. Add queso fresco, cilantro, pickled red onions, lettuce, and mayo, or other fixings and condiments. Serve with a grilled jalapeño.

LOMO SALTADO

SERVES 4

- **1 tablespoon ají amarillo paste**
- **2 tablespoons soy sauce**
- **1 tablespoon red wine vinegar**
- **1 tablespoon oyster sauce**
- **¼ cup Smoky Beef Tallow (page 43), divided**
- **1 pound teres major steaks, silverskin removed, cut into ½-inch chunks**
- **3 to 4 green onions, green parts trimmed, cut and chopped into 1-inch pieces**
- **1 medium red onion, sliced**
- **1 cup heirloom cherry tomatoes, halved**
- **1 tablespoon Smoke-Roasted Garlic (page 46)**
- **1 tablespoon minced fresh ginger**
- **1 teaspoon kosher salt**
- **1 teaspoon finely ground black pepper**
- **2 tablespoons chopped cilantro leaves**
- **Cooked rice, Crispy Beef Tallow–Roasted Potatoes (page 147), or french fries, for serving**

This signature Peruvian stir-fry combines Asian influence with native ingredients. I'm a huge lover of Peru and Peruvian food, and this is an iconic dish from Lima, Peru.

French fries are usually tossed in the dish toward the end. I've never really cared for that, as I don't like the "soggy fries" texture. On a visit to Lima, I had a version with roasted potatoes that worked much better for my palate, and that's what I'm going with here.

***Lomo* translates to "loin" or "tenderloin" in English, and this dish is usually made with beef tenderloin or another tender cut. If I'm using beef, I like to use teres major in this dish, as it's very tender but also has a bit more flavor than tenderloin. You can also use cuts such as New York strip or skirt steak, but be aware that they can get pretty tough and chewy if overcooked.**

This is best cooked in a wok over screaming-high heat. Cook the ingredients in small batches to keep your wok hot so the food sears instead of steams.

In a bowl, whisk together the ají amarillo paste, soy sauce, vinegar, and oyster sauce. Set aside.

Line a plate with a paper towel. Heat a wok or a high-sided skillet over medium-high heat. Place ⅛ cup of the beef tallow in the skillet and heat. Then add the beef in batches. Sear the pieces for 1 minute, then toss and cook for another 30 seconds. Transfer to a plate, then cook the remaining beef.

Heat the remaining ⅛ cup of beef tallow in the pan. Add the green onions and sear for 30 seconds, then add the red onion and cook for 1 minute while stirring. Add the tomatoes and cook until blistered. Add the garlic and ginger and toss lightly, then add the sauce and beef. Cook for 2 minutes, letting the sauce coat the beef and vegetables. Add the salt and pepper, toss in the cilantro, and stir to incorporate. Serve with Crispy Beef Tallow–Roasted Potatoes (page 147).

6

POULTRY

SMOKED CHICKEN WITH VINEGAR BBQ SAUCE

SERVES 4

Smoked Chicken

2 (2-pound) half chickens

½ tablespoon olive oil

2 tablespoons Classic BBQ Rub (page 38)

Vinegar BBQ Sauce

Makes about 4 cups

1 cup apple cider vinegar

1 cup red wine vinegar

2 cups ketchup

1 cup brown sugar

2 tablespoons coarsely ground black pepper

1 tablespoon smoked paprika

2 teaspoons granulated garlic

2 teaspoons salt

2 teaspoons red pepper flakes

I often tell people, if you're going to smoke one chicken, you may as well smoke two and pull the leftovers. Hand-pulled smoked chicken is a game changer for delicious meals such as chicken salad, chicken potpie, chicken and dumplings, wraps, salads, and more. Smoked chicken is simple. I'm using half chickens for this recipe, but you can cook them whole and/or spatchcocked simply by adjusting your cooking time.

Prepare a smoker to cook at 275°F with applewood or cherrywood. Place the half chickens on a sheet pan and pat dry with paper towels. Rub both sides with the olive oil, then season with the rub. Cook in the smoker for 2 hours, or until the internal temperature of the breast reaches 160°F.

While the chicken is cooking, prepare the sauce. Place all the ingredients in a small saucepan over medium-low heat. Whisk occasionally and cook until the brown sugar is dissolved, about 5 minutes. The sauce will keep in the fridge for up to 2 weeks.

Remove the chicken from the smoker, cover, and let rest for 5 minutes. Serve with the sauce.

DUCK BREASTS WITH SMOKED BLUEBERRY MOSTARDA

SERVES 4

Smoked Blueberry Mostarda

Makes about 1½ cups

- 2 cups fresh blueberries
- 1 tablespoon olive oil
- 1 small shallot, minced
- 1 tablespoon finely chopped fresh rosemary
- 1 teaspoon sugar
- Kosher salt and finely ground black pepper
- 3 tablespoons Champagne Mustard (page 47)
- 1 teaspoon champagne vinegar or white wine vinegar
- Dash of fresh lemon juice
- 1 teaspoon lemon zest

Duck Breasts

- 2 tablespoons kosher salt
- 1 tablespoon coarsely ground black pepper
- 2 teaspoons granulated garlic
- 2 teaspoons paprika
- 1 teaspoon granulated onion
- 1 teaspoon dried oregano
- ½ teaspoon crushed red pepper flakes
- 4 (8-ounce) skin-on duck breasts

A juicy medium-rare duck breast with crispy skin is a wonderful dish. It's even better when it's imbued with the extra flavor meat gets when cooked on the grill. But it's absolutely fantastic when you serve it with a flavorful sauce. Mostarda is an Italian sauce that features dried or fresh fruit and mustard. It ends up being a sweet and spicy sauce. For the fruit in this version, I smoke fresh blueberries before cooking the sauce.

(continued)

To make the mostarda, preheat a smoker to 250°F. Smoke the blueberries in an aluminum pan for 20 to 30 minutes.

Heat the olive oil in a saucepan over medium heat, add the shallot, and sauté until softened, about 3 minutes. Add the blueberries, rosemary, and sugar and season with salt and pepper to taste. Stir occasionally and cook until the blueberries start to break down. (They will thicken into a jammy consistency in about 8 minutes.) Stir in the mustard and cook for another 2 to 3 minutes. Remove from the heat and add the vinegar, lemon juice, and lemon zest. Cool slightly before serving.

To make the duck, mix together all the ingredients except the duck breasts in a small bowl. Using paper towels, pat the duck breasts dry, then lightly score the skin in a crisscross pattern. (Take your time and don't cut through the fat or the meat juices will render and ruin the crispiness of the skin. I try to cut my crisscross lines very small so I'll get more rendering.) Season the duck breasts with the blend and place on a wire rack over a sheet pan. Refrigerate, skin side up, for 4 to 8 hours.

Prepare a grill with a two-zone fire with 2 to 3 cherrywood chunks, with one fully lit chimney of charcoal on one side of the grill. Brush and oil the grates.

Place the duck breasts, skin side down, in a cool cast-iron pan and place the pan in the cool area of the grill. Cover the grill, checking on the duck breasts every 5 minutes to keep an eye on the rendering process. Fully rendering the fat should take 12 to 20 minutes, depending on the grill temperature. (If the fat is bubbling and popping, it's too hot; you'll need to remove the breasts and let the grill cool a bit.) Cook until the skin is rendered, golden brown, and crispy. Using a spatula, lift one breast and allow as much fat as possible to drain off. Place it, meat side down, over the coals. Repeat with the remaining breasts. Cook until the internal temperature registers 130°F, 2 to 3 minutes. Remove the breasts from the grill, cover, and let rest for 5 minutes.

For each serving, plate ¼ of the mostarda and place a duck breast over it.

BUTTERMILK FRIED CHICKEN

SERVES 4 TO 6

Marinade

2 cups buttermilk

2 cups hot sauce

½ cup SPG+ Seasoning (page 45)

Fried Chicken

1 (4-pound) whole chicken, cut into 8 frying pieces

2 cups canola oil

Seasoned Flour

4 cups self-rising flour

½ cup SPG+ Seasoning (page 45)

This recipe really speaks from the heart of Mississippi, taking a common item, treating it in a simple yet very flavorful manner, and serving it hot and crispy. For a true Delta rendition, use a cast-iron skillet. The seasoned flour is my go-to for frying just about anything, and I keep it in the pantry. I typically fry chicken in batches according to the sizes of the pieces. I cook the wings with the breasts and then the thighs with the legs. An instant-read thermometer is great for checking the temperature of both the oil and the chicken. Serve with Pikliz (page 146) and Baked Beans from Scratch (page 148).

To make the marinade, place the buttermilk, hot sauce, and seasoning in a large bowl and stir lightly to combine.

To make the fried chicken, coat the chicken thoroughly with the marinade, cover, and refrigerate for 8 to 12 hours, stirring occasionally.

Line a plate with a paper towel. In a large cast-iron skillet over medium-high heat, heat the canola oil to 350°F. To make the seasoned flour, on a large plate, stir together the flour and seasoning. One piece at a time, remove the chicken from the marinade, shake off any excess liquid, and dredge in the seasoned flour, making sure all sides are coated. First place the breasts in the skillet and fry for 1 minute. Add the wings and cook for at least 3 to 4 minutes before turning. Cook for about 2 more minutes, or until the internal temperature is over 165°F in the breasts.

Transfer the pieces to the paper towel–lined plate. Place the thighs and legs in the skillet and cook for 3 to 4 minutes, then turn and cook for another 3 to 4 minutes, or until the internal temperature registers 175°F in the thighs. Transfer to the plate and serve.

ACHIOTE ROTISSERIE CHICKEN

SERVES 2 TO 4

- **4 dried guajillo chiles**
- **1 to 2 dried chile de árbol (optional)**
- **1½ cups water, divided**
- **2 ounces achiote paste or achiote powder**
- **4 cloves garlic, peeled and smashed**
- **1 tablespoon paprika**
- **½ cup orange juice**
- **1 teaspoon minced fresh oregano leaves**
- **¼ cup coarsely chopped cilantro leaves**
- **1 teaspoon ground cumin**
- **1 teaspoon kosher salt**
- **1 tablespoon extra-virgin olive oil**
- **1 (4-pound) whole chicken**

Achiote paste (and sometimes powder) can be found in Hispanic markets or in some grocery stores with a strong ethnic section. It has an earthy, slightly peppery taste that really works well in tandem with orange juice, garlic, and guajillo chiles. Achiote paste is made from annatto seeds, which are often used to color foods with a beautiful red hue.

While I love the flavor of a rotisserie-cooked bird, this recipe works for chicken pieces, either grilled or roasted, pork chops, and even baby back ribs.

In a small saucepan over medium-high heat, toast the guajillo chiles and chile de árbol for 4 to 5 minutes, being careful not to let them burn. Add 1 cup of the water, bring to a boil, then lower to a simmer for 5 minutes. Remove the pan from the heat and let cool, then stem and seed.

Place the chiles, remaining ½ cup of water, achiote paste, garlic, paprika, orange juice, oregano, cilantro, cumin, salt, and olive oil in a blender and pulse until puréed.

Wearing gloves, coat the chicken inside and out with the mixture. Loosen the skin around the breasts and thighs and work some of the marinade under the skin. Place the chicken in a pan, cover with plastic wrap, and marinate for at least 4 hours.

Prepare a grill with a rotisserie attachment to cook at around 400°F to 420°F. Place lit coals on the sides and set a disposable aluminum pan in the center of the grill.

Truss and skewer the chicken. Place on the rotisserie grill and cook for 1 hour, or until an instant-read thermometer inserted in the breast registers 160°F. Remove the chicken from the grill, let rest for 10 to 15 minutes, and carve to serve.

CORNISH GAME HENS WITH SMOKY RED PEPPER GLAZE

SERVES 2

Red Pepper Jam

Makes 6 half-pint jars

18 to 20 red jalapeños, seeded and diced

1 red bell pepper, diced

Olive oil

1 head garlic, top quarter cut off

2 cups apple cider vinegar, divided

1 teaspoon kosher salt

1 (1.75-ounce) packet powdered pectin

5 cups sugar

Cornish Game Hens

2 (1-pound) Cornish game hens, thawed

2 tablespoons SPG+ Seasoning (page 45)

½ tablespoon turbinado or brown sugar

Red Pepper Glaze

¾ cup Red Pepper Jam

¼ cup apple cider vinegar

1 tablespoon brown sugar

1 tablespoon Dijon mustard

1 teaspoon kosher salt

1 teaspoon minced fresh rosemary

½ teaspoon coarsely ground black pepper

¼ teaspoon crushed red pepper flakes

Cornish game hens are not actual game birds but young chickens that usually weigh between 1 and 2 pounds. They are very tender and make for a pretty plate presentation. Depending on appetites, serve one per two people or one per person. Poultry doesn't have red meat's collagens and connective tissue, so the only reason to cook it low and slow is to add more smoke flavor. My go-to poultry cooking temperature is 275°F to 325°F.

Every year I grow a few plants in raised beds on my patio, and I always grow jalapeño pepper plants. I love to let jalapeños ripen to a beautiful red color and then make my red pepper jam. It's amazing over smoked cream cheese with crackers or in a spicy-sweet glaze for these smoked Cornish game hens. It also works well with salmon or pork.

(continued)

To make the jam, prepare a smoker to cook at 275°F. Place the jalapeños and bell pepper on a large sheet pan, drizzle with olive oil, then turn the peppers to coat. Add the garlic and drizzle a bit more olive oil on the cut end. Place the pan in the smoker and cook for 40 to 45 minutes, turning the peppers after 20 minutes.

Remove the pan from the smoker and let cool. Seed the peppers, then place them in a food processor. Squeeze the garlic cloves into the processor, add 1 cup of the vinegar, then purée.

Place the purée in a large pot with the remaining 1 cup of vinegar and the salt and pectin. Bring to a boil, then add the sugar, stirring occasionally. Once the sugar has dissolved, after 4 to 5 minutes, turn off the heat and ladle the jam into jelly jars. (I usually use half-pint jars.)

If canning, follow these additional steps:

Put the lids and rings on the jars. (Do not overtighten the rings.) Place the jars in a canner with boiling water, then bring back to a boil. Keep at a boil for at least 5 minutes. Remove the jars and let cool. If any do not "pop," repeat the process or refrigerate and use within 1 week.

To prepare the hens, use paper towels to pat them dry inside and out. Tuck the wing tips behind the drummettes to form a triangle. (This helps the bird stay upright.) Mix the seasoning with the sugar, then season the hens inside and out and tie the legs together. Place a wire rack on a sheet pan, set the hens on top, and place the pan in the fridge. Dry-brine the hens overnight.

Prepare a smoker to cook at 275°F with 2 to 3 chunks of fruit wood. (Cherrywood is my favorite to use for game hens.) Place the hens on the smoker with a meat thermometer in the thickest part of the breast. Cook for 1 hour 15 minutes, or until the temperature registers 160°F.

While the hens are cooking, prepare the glaze. Place all the ingredients in a small saucepan over medium heat. Whisk to incorporate as the jelly melts. Cook for 5 minutes, or until the sugar is dissolved. Taste and adjust the seasoning as needed.

Brush the hens with the glaze and cook for 3 minutes to set the glaze. Remove the hens from the smoker and let rest for 10 minutes. Serve with additional glaze on the side.

SICHUAN PEPPERCORN CHICKEN BREASTS WITH SEARED PLUMS AND PEPPERS

SERVES 4

- 2 tablespoons Sichuan peppercorns
- ½ tablespoon kosher salt
- 4 (6-ounce) boneless skinless chicken breasts
- 1½ tablespoons sesame oil
- 1 clove garlic, minced
- ¼ cup chopped red onion
- ½ tablespoon minced fresh ginger
- ½ poblano, roasted, seeded, and diced
- 6 plums, peeled, pitted, and quartered
- 1 cup chicken stock
- 2 teaspoons fresh thyme leaves
- 4 tablespoons salted butter
- 2 tablespoons soy sauce
- ½ teaspoon red pepper flakes
- 1½ tablespoons honey
- Cooked rice, for serving

Most people cut chicken into chunks when cooking with Chinese or Japanese flavors, à la stir-fry. For this dish, however, I love cooking whole breasts crusted with crushed Sichuan peppers on one side and finished on a grill. The seared plums and peppers nicely counteract the spiciness of the peppercorns. Serve this with a side of rice and you have a quick, delicious meal.

Prepare a grill to medium heat with a two-zone fire. Warm a cast-iron skillet on the grill. Place the peppercorns in the skillet and toast for 2 to 3 minutes, then transfer to a mortar and lightly crack with a pestle. Mix the peppercorns with the salt, then coat one side of each chicken breast.

Add the sesame oil to the skillet, then add the chicken breasts and cook for 3 to 4 minutes, or until seared. Flip the breasts over, cook for 5 minutes, then remove to a plate.

Place the garlic, onion, ginger, poblano, and plums in the skillet. Sear for 3 minutes, then stir. Add the chicken stock, stir, and cook until the stock is reduced by half. Add the thyme, butter, soy sauce, red pepper flakes, and honey and cook until thickened. Remove the skillet from the grill, place a quarter of the sauce on a plate, then lay a breast over the sauce. Repeat with the remaining sauce and breasts. Serve with rice or your favorite side dish.

"PERUVIAN" SMOKED CHICKEN WITH AJÍ VERDE SAUCE

SERVES 2 TO 4

Ají Verde Sauce

Makes about 2½ cups

- 1 cup packed cilantro leaves
- ½ cup mayonnaise
- 2 jalapeños, roasted, seeded, blistered, skin removed, and chopped (add another jalapeño or hotter peppers if you like it spicy)
- ½ tablespoon Smoke-Roasted Garlic (page 46) or minced garlic
- 1 tablespoon extra-virgin olive oil
- Juice and finely grated zest of 1 lime
- 2 tablespoons ají amarillo paste
- ½ teaspoon salt
- ½ cup grated Cotija or Parmesan
- ⅛ teaspoon finely ground black pepper

Marinade

- 1 tablespoon granulated garlic
- 1 tablespoon ground cumin
- 1 tablespoon kosher salt
- 1 tablespoon smoked paprika or mild paprika
- ½ tablespoon fresh Mexican oregano, coarsely chopped
- ¾ tablespoon coarsely ground black pepper
- 2 teaspoons granulated onion
- 1 teaspoon cayenne pepper
- 1 teaspoon fresh thyme leaves
- 1 teaspoon dried basil
- 2 to 3 tablespoons extra-virgin olive oil

Chicken

- 1 (3½-pound) whole chicken

Since I started writing cookbooks and my blog, I hope I've helped some aspiring cooks and barbecuers. I've often said "there's always pizza" in case my culinary experiments go wrong, so don't feel bad if something you're cooking doesn't turn out perfectly. It's okay, live and learn, and order a pizza!

Since I published this recipe years ago on my blog (MelissaCookston.com), it has been the top recipe. I cook this updated version often at home.

If you are a "sauce person," as I am, you will love the ají verde sauce. Cotija cheese has a fairly salty flavor, so feel free to season the sauce to your taste. For the best flavor, make the sauce a few hours before serving to allow the flavors to meld. It keeps for 5 to 6 days in the fridge and is great on anything from raw veggies to grilled steaks.

I prefer to use a smaller air-chilled whole chicken, so be sure to adjust your cooking time as necessary for the size of your bird.

Make the sauce a few hours before serving to allow the flavors to meld. Place all the ingredients in a blender, pulse until incorporated, then purée for 30 to 45 seconds.

To make the marinade, combine all the ingredients except the olive oil in a bowl. Add just enough olive oil to make a paste. Trim any extraneous fat or skin from the chicken, then pat dry with paper towels. Place the chicken, breast side down, on a cutting board. Using kitchen shears, cut out the backbone. Using a sharp knife, lightly slice the wishbone in the middle of the breast, then press the chicken flat.

Place the chicken in a large resealable plastic bag. Pour the marinade over the chicken, then squeeze as much air out of the bag as possible and seal. Marinate in the refrigerator for 8 to 24 hours.

Prepare a grill to medium-hot with a two-zone fire. If using a kettle grill, use one full standard-size charcoal chimney of lit charcoal. Put the charcoal and 2 to 3 chunks of cherrywood or pecan wood on one half of the grill.

Remove the chicken from the bag and pat with paper towels to remove any excess marinade from the chicken. Discard the marinade. Tuck the wing tips behind the drummettes to form a triangle. Place the chicken, skin side up, on the cooler side of the grill, with the legs toward the heat, and insert a meat thermometer into the thickest part of the breast. Cook for 45 minutes to 1 hour, or until the meat thermometer registers 125°F. Flip the chicken over, skin side down, and move to the hotter part of the grill. Cover the grill and to cook until the thermometer registers 160°F. Remove the chicken from the grill, let rest for 10 to 15 minutes, portion, and drizzle with the sauce.

GRILLED QUAIL WITH CHERMOULA

SERVES 4

Chermoula

Makes 1 cup

- 2 teaspoon ground coriander
- 2 teaspoon ground cumin
- 1 tablespoon Smoke-Roasted Garlic (page 46) or minced garlic
- 1 teaspoon smoked paprika
- ½ teaspoon grated fresh ginger
- Finely grated zest of ½ lemon
- Juice of 1 lemon, about 3 tablespoons
- ½ teaspoon crushed red pepper flakes
- 1 cup cilantro leaves
- 1 cup Italian parsley leaves
- ½ cup fresh mint leaves
- 1 teaspoon kosher salt
- ¾ cup extra-virgin olive oil

Quail

- 8 Pharaoh quail, butterflied, roughly 4 ounces each

My grandfathers and my husband's grandfathers loved to go quail hunting. I still remember having fried bobwhites many times, so I keep a fond place in my heart for the little game birds. Most of the quail you can buy at the grocery store will be Coturnix, or Pharaoh, quail. Bobwhites are larger and have white meat for breasts, whereas Pharaoh breasts are dark meat. Quail is a small and thin game bird, so it will take only 5 to 7 minutes per side to grill. Quail is generally sold frozen and butterflied, so thaw overnight before using.

Chermoula is like chimichurri but with warmer North African spices. It's delicious on so many things, and you'll always love having it around. Use it to marinate a steak or chicken, top some hummus, on fish, or as a pasta sauce; serve it with grilled eggplant or dip bread; mix it with mayo for a salad dressing; and so much more. Its versatility is why it is one of my favorite condiments.

To make the chermoula, place all the ingredients in a food processor and pulse a few times to incorporate. Taste and adjust the salt. The chermoula will keep in the fridge for 2 to 3 days.

To prepare the quail, wearing gloves, place the quail on a sheet pan and pat dry with paper towels. Pour about half the chermoula in a container and reserve. Using your hands, apply the remaining chermoula to both sides of each bird. Cover and let sit for 30 minutes.

Prepare a grill to medium heat (around 375°F). Add 2 to 3 chunks of applewood to the outside of the fire. Place the quail on the grill and cook for 5 to 7 minutes. Flip the quail and cook for another 5 to 7 minutes, or until the temperature reaches 165°F in the thickest part of the bird. Serve with the reserved chermoula on the side.

JERK CHICKEN THIGHS WITH TOMATO-SPICED BEANS AND RICE

SERVES 4

Jerk Seasoning

1 tablespoon granulated garlic

1 tablespoon granulated onion

½ tablespoon kosher salt

1 tablespoon brown sugar

½ tablespoon coarsely ground black pepper

1 teaspoon cayenne pepper (more if you want it hotter, less if you don't)

1 teaspoon ground ginger

1 teaspoon dried thyme

1 teaspoon ground allspice

1 teaspoon smoked paprika

½ teaspoon ground cinnamon

½ teaspoon ground nutmeg

½ teaspoon ground cumin

Chicken Thighs

2 pounds chicken thighs, preferably air-chilled

2 tablespoons extra-virgin olive oil, plus more for the grill

1½ to 2 tablespoons Jerk Seasoning

Tomato-Spiced Beans and Rice

Makes 2 quarts

2 tablespoons extra-virgin olive oil

1 medium yellow onion, diced

½ medium green bell pepper, diced

2 cloves garlic, peeled, smashed, and chopped

2 cups long-grain white rice

1 (14.5-ounce) can fire-roasted tomatoes

3 cups chicken or vegetable stock

2 (15.5-ounce) cans black beans, drained and rinsed

½ tablespoon minced Italian parsley leaves

2 teaspoons Smoked Tomato Powder (page 48)

1 teaspoon paprika

1 jalapeño, seeded and minced

1½ teaspoons kosher salt

1 teaspoon chipotle powder

1 teaspoon chopped fresh oregano leaves or ½ teaspoon dried oregano

½ teaspoon black pepper

1 to 2 teaspoons Herb Oil (page 42) (optional)

(continued)

My foundation, the World Junior BBQ League, has several aspiring pitmasters in the Caribbean. The Grand Cayman chapter has led the way, and I've traveled there several times. The kids there cook great food, but you can tell when they're cooking in a contest in the Caymans versus one in the United States: They really pile on the island flavors, and it's fantastic, if spicy. Jerk seasoning is as ubiquitous in the Caribbean as BBQ rub is in the South. My version of jerk seasoning is mainly developed for chicken but also works well with snapper or pork.

There are lots of jerk seasoning recipes, with just about every household on the islands having their own "secret perfect recipe." I like to think of jerk seasoning as more of a warm, nutty flavor that will put you in a relaxing mood. Maybe it's the island talking, but I always calm down with a nice piece of jerk chicken served with tomato-spiced beans and rice. Now, who has the piña coladas?

To make the seasoning, thoroughly mix together all the ingredients in a bowl.

To prepare the chicken, place the chicken thighs on a sheet pan, drizzle with the olive oil, then add enough seasoning to coat both sides. Using a fork or a forty-eight-blade meat tenderizer, tenderize the thighs on both sides to help force the seasoning into the meat. Cover the thighs with plastic wrap and marinate for 20 to 30 minutes or overnight in the fridge.

Prepare a medium-high heat grill with a two-zone fire. Brush and oil the grates. Place the thighs, skin side down, on the hotter part of the grill. Cover and cook until the skin has grill marks and is browned, 8 to 10 minutes. Flip the thighs over and cook until they register 175°F on a meat thermometer, 10 to 12 minutes. Move the thighs to the cooler side of the grill if necessary to avoid burning.

To make the beans and rice, heat the olive oil in a large frying pan with a tight-fitting lid over medium-high heat. Add the onion and bell pepper and cook for 6 to 7 minutes, or until softened. Add the garlic and cook for 2 minutes, or until fragrant. Stir in the rice and cook for 3 to 4 minutes to toast, then add the remaining ingredients except the herb oil, if using. Stir to incorporate while bringing to a boil. Decrease the heat to medium-low, then cover and cook for 25 minutes, or until the liquids are absorbed and the rice is tender. Season with salt and pepper to taste, drizzle with the herb oil, if using, and serve.

SAUCY ADOBO WINGS WITH HERBY BUTTERMILK DRESSING

SERVES 4

Adobo Seasoning

1 tablespoon kosher salt

1 tablespoon smoked paprika

2 teaspoons coarsely ground black pepper

2 teaspoons ancho chili powder

1 teaspoon granulated garlic

1 teaspoon onion powder

1 teaspoon dried Mexican oregano

1 teaspoon ground cumin

Chicken Wings

1 pound whole chicken wings

¼ cup neutral oil, such as peanut oil

Sauce

1½ cups mild hot sauce, such as Cholula

1 cup (2 sticks) salted butter, melted

Juice of 1 lime

½ tablespoon granulated garlic

1 teaspoon ground cumin

1 teaspoon chipotle powder

1 teaspoon coarsely ground black pepper

2 tablespoons chopped cilantro leaves

1 teaspoon cayenne pepper (optional; more for spicier wings)

1 to 2 tablespoons avocado oil

Herby Buttermilk Dressing (recipe follows), for serving

(continued)

I love a good saucy wing. This version takes some inspiration from south of the border and uses my adobo seasoning blend on the chicken wings. I don't care for burn-your-mouth hot sauces, so I use a relatively mild one for this recipe, but feel free to use your favorite. You can also add more spice if desired.

To prepare the seasoning, mix all the ingredients together in a bowl.

To make the chicken, prepare a smoker to cook at 275°F. Pat the wings dry with a paper towel, then toss with the oil and season thoroughly with the adobo seasoning. Place the wings in the smoker and cook, turning once, for 1½ hours, or until the internal temperature registers 185°F.

While the wings are cooking, to make the sauce, place all the ingredients in a large bowl and whisk to incorporate.

Remove the wings from the smoker, toss in the sauce, and serve with the Herby Buttermilk Dressing.

HERBY BUTTERMILK DRESSING

Makes 2½ cups

1 cup Bulgarian-style buttermilk

1 cup mayonnaise

2 tablespoons minced fresh tarragon leaves

2 tablespoons minced red onion

1 tablespoon minced fresh Italian parsley leaves

1 tablespoon minced fresh dill or ½ tablespoon dried dill

1 teaspoon Smoke-Roasted Garlic (page 46)

1 teaspoon coarsely ground black pepper

1 teaspoon kosher salt

1 teaspoon hot sauce, such as Louisiana brand

Finely grated zest of 1 lemon

Ranch dressing is America's favorite salad dressing. People use it for salads, dips, and, heck, even pizza. I don't go that far, but I do love a good buttermilk dressing now and then. I am not taking sides on the "mayo wars" here. Duke's, Hellman's, or Blue Plate will all produce a fine dressing. However, if you want to have restaurant-quality dressing, get some "heavy-duty mayo."

In a mixing bowl, whisk together all the ingredients to incorporate. Taste and adjust the salt and pepper as needed. The dressing will keep for 5 days in the fridge.

7

SEAFOOD/FISH

FRIED CATFISH WITH TARTAR SAUCE

SERVES 2

Tartar Sauce

Makes 1½ cups

1 cup mayonnaise

2 tablespoons sweet pickle relish

1 tablespoon finely diced yellow onion

1½ teaspoons fresh lemon juice

Pinch of kosher salt

Pinch of coarsely ground black pepper

Fried Catfish

Canola oil, for frying

2 cups self-rising yellow cornmeal

1 tablespoon coarsely ground black pepper

2 tablespoons SPG+ Seasoning (page 45)

4 (5 to 7-ounce) catfish fillets

1 cup buttermilk

Yellow onion slices or whole scallions, for serving

Mississippi farm-raised catfish is the best in the world. I'm not sure why, but I am sure that the folks in the Delta know their catfish. Farm-raised catfish tastes clean, with a nice flaky texture when cooked correctly, and will compare favorably to much more expensive fish. In Mississippi, it's traditional to serve catfish with a slice of yellow onion or a whole scallion.

To make the tartar sauce, place all the ingredients in a small mixing bowl and whisk well.

Heat 2 inches of the canola oil in a large skillet or a deep fryer heated to 350°F. Line a plate with paper towels. Place the cornmeal, pepper, and seasoning on a large plate and mix well. Rinse the fillets, pat them dry, and then lightly dust them with the cornmeal mixture. Dredge the fillets through the buttermilk, then place them in the cornmeal mixture and press lightly to make sure the cornmeal sticks. Flip the fillets and press lightly.

Gently lay each fillet in the hot oil and cook for 2 to 3 minutes, then flip and cook for another 2 to 3 minutes, or until the coating is crunchy and the fish is cooked thoroughly.

Place the fillets on the plate to drain, then serve with the tartar sauce on the side and a slice of yellow onion or a whole scallion.

CRAB CAKES WITH MISSISSIPPI COMEBACK SAUCE

MAKES 4 CRAB CAKES

Mississippi Comeback Sauce

Makes about 2 cups

¼ cup chili sauce

1 tablespoon finely diced red onion

1½ teaspoons minced garlic

¼ cup ketchup

1 tablespoon Worcestershire sauce

1 teaspoon whole-grain mustard

1 cup mayonnaise

1 teaspoon coarsely ground black pepper

1 teaspoon hot sauce, such as Louisiana brand

Juice of ½ lemon

Crab Cakes

¼ cup mayonnaise

1 egg

1 tablespoon whole-grain mustard

1 teaspoon fresh lemon juice

½ teaspoon kosher salt

½ teaspoon black pepper

1 tablespoon finely chopped fresh Italian parsley leaves

1 tablespoon finely chopped scallion (green and white parts)

1 pound jumbo lump crabmeat

⅓ cup panko breadcrumbs

1 tablespoon salted butter, melted

1½ teaspoons Delta Creole Seasoning (page 37)

It's not hard to talk me into a crab cake, especially these! These aren't your typical heavily breaded crab cakes. The crab is really the star in this recipe, which is one reason I splurge to get the jumbo lump crabmeat when I'm making these.

Mississippi Comeback Sauce is a "kissing cousin" to rémoulade. This version has a bit of a kick that goes nicely with crab cakes or any type of seafood. In the words of the Beverly Hillbillies, "Y'all come back now, ya hear?"

To make the sauce, whisk all the ingredients together in a small bowl. Cover and refrigerate for 30 minutes before serving. Store in an airtight container in the refrigerator for up to 5 days.

To make the crab cakes, place the mayonnaise, egg, mustard, lemon juice, salt, pepper, parsley, and scallion in a medium mixing bowl. Gently fold in the crab and panko, breaking up the crab as little as possible. Refrigerate the mixture for 30 minutes.

Heat a grill to high heat. On a sheet pan, form the crab mixture into 4 mounds. (You can use a half-cup measuring cup to give you an idea of the right size.) Lightly press down on each mound, being careful not to break up the crab pieces. Brush each one with the butter and lightly sprinkle with the seasoning.

Place the sheet pan on the grill and cook for 5 to 8 minutes, until the crab cakes are hot and slightly browned. Remove the pan from the grill and use a thin metal spatula to carefully remove the crab cakes from the pan. Plate and serve with the sauce on the side.

DEFINITELY NOT TRADITIONAL CREOLE CRAWFISH ÉTOUFFÉE

SERVES 3 TO 4

- **4 tablespoons (½ stick) salted butter**
- **4 tablespoons all-purpose flour**
- **1 medium yellow onion, diced**
- **1 green bell pepper, diced**
- **3 ribs celery, diced**
- **2 teaspoons minced garlic**
- **8 ounces chicken bone broth**
- **1 tablespoon Delta Creole Seasoning (page 37)**
- **2 bay leaves**
- **1 (14-ounce) can fire-roasted tomatoes**
- **1 tablespoon gochujang**
- **1 tablespoon soy sauce**
- **½ teaspoon coarsely ground black pepper**
- **Kosher salt**
- **1 pound peeled crawfish tails**
- **1 tablespoon chopped Italian parsley leaves**
- **Cooked rice, for serving**
- **1 tablespoon chopped green onions, for serving**

Crawfish étouffée is a classic Louisiana dish. This recipe is not a classic but rather a take on one. Most traditional Louisiana dishes have two versions: Creole and Cajun. Creole dishes are more herbaceous and contain tomatoes; Cajun dishes don't contain tomatoes and have a spicier edge. I prefer the Creole version, with some adjustments. However, I'm only very nominally following any tradition for this version. I add some gochujang and soy sauce for spice and umami flavors and fire-roasted tomatoes instead of the traditional Creole diced tomatoes. I use bone broth instead of chicken broth, which adds some protein and creates a silkier texture. While crawfish étouffée is usually served with rice, it is also a flavorful pasta dish. Save and freeze any leftovers, then warm up and use as a sauce over a piece of seared fish or chicken another day for a very decadent, easy dinner.

In a heavy-bottomed stockpot, melt the butter over medium heat and whisk in the flour to make a roux, stirring constantly so it doesn't burn. Cook for 5 to 10 minutes, or until caramel-colored. (You don't want a super dark roux for this dish.)

Add the onion, bell pepper, and celery and cook for 4 to 5 minutes. Add the garlic and cook for another 2 minutes. Slowly whisk in the bone broth a few ounces at a time. Add the seasoning, bay leaves, tomatoes, gochujang, soy sauce, pepper, and salt to taste and stir to combine. Bring to a boil, then decrease the heat to medium-low, cover, and simmer for 15 minutes. Add the crawfish tails and cook for 3 to 4 minutes. Remove from the heat, stir in the parsley, and adjust the seasoning. Serve with rice garnished with green onions.

BUTCHER PAPER SMOKED TUNA SALAD WITH AVOCADO GREEN GODDESS DRESSING

SERVES 2

Avocado Green Goddess Dressing

Makes 1½ cups

¾ cup whole-milk Greek yogurt

¼ cup water

1 avocado, mashed

1 teaspoon Smoke-Roasted Garlic (page 46) or minced garlic

1 cup Italian parsley leaves

2 tablespoons minced fresh chives

2 tablespoons minced fresh cilantro leaves

2 tablespoons minced fresh tarragon leaves

¼ teaspoon salt

¼ teaspoon coarsely ground black pepper

Zest of ½ lemon

Juice of 1 lemon

Smoked Tuna Salad

1 tablespoon minced fresh parsley leaves

2 teaspoon salt

½ teaspoon coarsely ground black pepper

½ teaspoon granulated garlic

1 teaspoon smoked paprika

3 tablespoons olive oil, divided

2 (5 to 6-ounce) yellowfin tuna steaks

1 medium yellow onion, slivered

½ red bell pepper, slivered

2 heads radicchio

1 English cucumber, thinly sliced

½ medium red onion, thinly sliced

1 avocado, peeled, pitted, and sliced

2 radishes or 1 watermelon radish, thinly sliced

(continued)

Back in the day, when we competed in BBQ contests every weekend, we lived a feast-or-famine life. Win, and steaks were on the menu. Get blanked, and tuna fish sandwiches would make up our lunches. After too many of those, I swore off tuna fish sandwiches—that is, until I decided to add some smoky and intense flavors and came up with my smoked tuna salad with green goddess dressing. Pink butcher paper is semi-porous and allows the smoke flavors into the paper, unlike parchment paper. Like cooking en papillote, however, it will help retain moisture as the tuna cooks.

I keep an herb garden year-round, though it shines in the summer. Green goddess dressing typically uses parsley, chives, and tarragon, but you can make this versatile dressing with any combination of herbs. Many recipes use a mixture of sour cream and mayo, but I like to use whole-milk Greek yogurt for more body. This dressing works amazingly as a dip for veggies or even fries; as a sandwich topping or salad dressing; or even drizzled over roasted veggies or chicken.

To make the dressing, place all the ingredients in a food processor and pulse until combined. Taste and adjust the seasoning as needed. Set aside.

To make the tuna salad, preheat a grill with a two-zone fire to medium-hot with 2 to 3 chunks of applewood. In a small bowl, mix together the parsley, salt, pepper, garlic, paprika, and 1 tablespoon of the olive oil. Pat the tuna steaks dry with paper towels, then rub all sides with the seasoning paste. Tear off a 2-foot section of 18-inch-wide pink butcher paper. Fold the paper into thirds, then place the yellow onion and bell pepper in the center section. Drizzle with 1 tablespoon of the olive oil, then place the seasoned tuna pieces on top of the vegetables. Fold over the two sides, then roll the paper up, tucking any excess under the packet.

Place the packet on the cool side of the grill and cook until the internal temperature registers 132°F to 135°F, about 30 to 45 minutes. Remove from the grill and thinly slice.

While the tuna is cooking, slice the radicchio and brush with the remaining 1 tablespoon of olive oil. Place the radicchio on the flame side of the grill and cook until slightly charred on the cut side and the exterior, about 5 minutes per side.

To serve, plate the radicchio in the center of a large platter. Place the cucumber, red onion, avocado, and radishes in a large bowl and add the dressing to coat. Toss to mix, then plate in the middle of the platter. Top with the smoked tuna slices and serve.

GRILLED CATFISH WITH CRAWFISH DRESSING AND THYME BEURRE BLANC

SERVES 4 TO 6

Cast-Iron Cornbread

Makes 1 (10-inch) cornbread

1 tablespoon neutral oil, such as peanut oil, for the pan

4 cups self-rising white cornmeal

1 cup self-rising flour

1 large egg

2 cups Bulgarian-style buttermilk

1 cup hot water

Crawfish Dressing

6 tablespoons salted butter

1 tablespoon diced celery

½ green bell pepper, diced

½ medium yellow onion, diced

1 tablespoon Smoke-Roasted Garlic (page 46)

1 pound Cast-Iron Cornbread

4 slices white bread, torn into ½-inch pieces

6 saltine crackers, crumbled

3 cups chicken stock

1 tablespoon Delta Creole Seasoning (page 37)

1 teaspoon dried sage

1 teaspoon dried oregano

½ teaspoon dried thyme

2 teaspoons kosher salt

1 teaspoon coarsely ground black pepper

½ pound crawfish tails

Thyme Beurre Blanc

1 cup (2 sticks) unsalted butter, cold, divided

¼ cup finely chopped shallots

¼ cup dry white wine

2 tablespoons white wine vinegar

⅓ cup heavy cream

Pinch of kosher salt

½ teaspoon fresh thyme leaves

Catfish

2 pounds boneless skinless catfish fillets

1 tablespoon olive oil

1 tablespoon Delta Creole Seasoning (page 37)

This dish is perfect for a tasty meal with family and friends. To me, it is Delta comfort food in a nutshell. Mississippi farm-raised catfish served over a cornbread-crawfish stuffing will warm your bones on a chilly night, and the simple Thyme Beurre Blanc ties everything together with a rich buttery kiss (and works amazingly well with any grilled fish or chicken breast).

If you make the cornbread for this recipe, enjoy up to two-thirds of it with a meal of fried pork chops, smoky turnip greens, and pinto beans (recipes on MelissaCookston.com). Cover the remaining one-third for this recipe with a paper towel and leave it out to dry until the next day.

You can also use this stuffing recipe to make a Southern Thanksgiving dressing. Just omit the crawfish and Delta Creole Seasoning and add plenty of sage.

To make the cornbread, place the oil in a cast-iron skillet and put the skillet in the oven. Preheat the oven to 450°F.

Mix the remaining ingredients in a bowl, then pour into the hot skillet. Bake for 20 to 25 minutes, or until the crust is golden brown and the bread is firm. Run a knife along the edge of the pan, then pry up and flip the cornbread in the skillet to keep the crust crispy. When cool, cover one-third of the cornbread and leave out to dry.

To make the dressing, preheat the oven to 350°F. In a medium pan over medium-high heat, melt 2 tablespoons of the butter, then add the celery, bell pepper, and onion until softened, 5 to 6 minutes. Add the garlic and cook for another 1 to 2 minutes.

Lightly crumble the cornbread and add it to a large mixing bowl with the white bread and crackers. Add the chicken stock, seasoning, herbs, cooked vegetables, salt, pepper, and crawfish tails. Mix thoroughly with your hands, then cover and let sit for 15 minutes. Pour the mixture into a 9 by 9-inch baking dish, top with the remaining 4 tablespoons of butter, and bake until golden brown, 45 minutes to 1 hour.

To make the beurre blanc, melt 1 tablespoon of the butter in a pan over medium heat. Add the shallots and whisk for 30 seconds. Add the wine and vinegar and cook until almost evaporated. Add the cream, salt, and thyme and bring to a boil while whisking. Decrease the heat to medium-low, then slowly whisk in the remaining butter 2 to 3 tablespoons at a time. Strain the sauce through a fine mesh strainer, using the back of a spoon to press the shallots to release their flavor.

To make the catfish, preheat a grill to medium-high heat. Brush and oil the grates. Brush the fillets with the olive oil, then sprinkle with the seasoning. Place the fillets on the grill and cook for 5 minutes on each side.

To serve, plate a portion of the dressing, place a fillet over it, and spoon some of the beurre blanc over the fish.

GRILLED RED SNAPPER WITH PISCO LIME SAUCE AND CORN MAQUE CHOUX

SERVES 4

Maque Choux

- 1 tablespoon bacon grease
- 1 tablespoon unsalted butter
- ¾ large yellow onion, diced
- ¾ red bell pepper, diced
- 1 to 2 jalapeños, seeded and diced
- 4 ears fresh corn, kernels cut off and cob scraped with a knife to release any "milk" (see method page 162)
- 1 teaspoon Delta Creole Seasoning (page 37)
- Kosher salt and freshly ground black pepper
- 1 cup heavy cream
- 2 teaspoons chopped fresh Italian parsley leaves

Pisco Lime Sauce

Makes ¾ cup

- 1 tablespoon olive oil
- ¼ small yellow onion, diced
- ¼ red bell pepper, diced
- ½ cup pisco or other brandy
- ¼ cup fresh lime juice (from about 2 limes)
- 1 tablespoon soy sauce
- 1 tablespoon brown sugar
- 1 tablespoon mirin
- 1 teaspoon Smoke-Roasted Garlic (page 46)
- Kosher salt and freshly ground black pepper
- 1 tablespoon chopped fresh cilantro leaves
- Finely grated zest of ½ lime

Grilled Red Snapper

- 1 teaspoon smoked paprika
- 1 teaspoon granulated garlic
- ½ teaspoon granulated onion
- ½ teaspoon black pepper
- ½ teaspoon dried thyme
- ½ teaspoon dried oregano
- ½ teaspoon salt
- ¼ teaspoon cayenne pepper (optional)
- 4 (5 to 6-ounce) skin-on red snapper fillets (thin fillets if possible)
- 1 to 3 teaspoons olive oil
- Peanut oil, for the grill grates

Many people don't like grilling fish as it's very easy to over- or undercook it, have it stick to the grill, or cook unevenly. Most of these issues are easily handled, and with some preparation, you'll love the extra flavor fish gets from the grill.

Always ensure your grill is very clean before you grill fish. Oil the grates right before cooking using tongs and paper towels soaked in peanut oil. The grill surface needs to be around 350°F or higher to properly cook the fish and keep it from drying out. I prefer to cook this recipe at 400°F. You can also use this recipe to cook salmon in a skillet.

(continued)

Pisco is a clear brandy that is claimed by both Peru and Chile. This recipe goes swimmingly well (see what I did there?) with a pisco sour (page 165).

Maque choux (pronounced *mock shoe*) is a corn-based dish predominantly served as a side. At its simplest, it is a blend of fresh corn, onions, bell pepper, milk or cream, and spices. Depending on the recipe, it may contain tomatoes. (This one doesn't.) It's easy to make and cooks in about 30 minutes.

To make the maque choux, heat the bacon grease and butter in a large skillet over medium-high heat. Add the onion, bell pepper, and jalapeño and cook for 6 to 8 minutes, or until the vegetables are softened. Add the corn, seasoning, and salt and pepper to taste and continue to cook for 4 to 5 minutes, or until the corn is hot and beginning to char. Decrease the heat to medium-low and add the cream. Stirring constantly, simmer until the cream has thickened, about 2 minutes. Stir in the parsley. Taste and adjust the seasoning as needed. Keep warm over very low heat until ready to serve.

To make the sauce, heat the olive oil in a saucepan over medium-high heat. Add the onion and bell pepper and cook until softened, 6 to 8 minutes. Add the pisco and cook for 2 to 3 minutes. Add the lime juice, soy sauce, brown sugar, mirin, garlic, and salt and pepper to taste. Bring to a boil, then let simmer and reduce until the sauce lightly coats the back of a spoon. Remove the pan from the heat and whisk in the cilantro and lime zest.

To make the snapper, preheat a grill to 400°F. In a small bowl, mix together the paprika, granulated garlic, granulated onion, pepper, thyme, oregano, salt, and cayenne pepper, if using. (Double the amount of cayenne pepper if you like it spicier.)

Let the snapper fillets come to room temperature for 15 minutes. Dry the fillets, then brush both sides with the olive oil. Season the fleshy side of the fillets with the seasoning blend and let sit for 5 minutes.

Brush the grill grates with peanut oil, then place the fillets skin side down on the grill. Close the lid and cook for 5 to 6 minutes. Open the lid and very carefully flip the fillets. Cook for another 2 to 3 minutes, until a meat thermometer registers 145°F in the center of the fillet.

Remove the fillets from the grill, drizzle with the sauce, and serve with the maque choux.

8

VEGGIES, SIDES, AND SUCH

GRAPE SALAD

SERVES 6 TO 8

- 1 cup sour cream
- 1 (8-ounce) package cream cheese, softened
- ½ cup granulated sugar
- 1 teaspoon vanilla extract
- 2 pounds seedless green grapes
- 2 pounds seedless red grapes
- 1 cup packed light brown sugar
- 1½ cups pecan halves

At the risk of being a little macabre, a whole lot of recipes make it through the South by being passed around at funerals. It's a tradition to make a dish and bring it to the home of the bereaved, and, of course, when the third cousin makes a delicious item, everyone has to get the recipe. That's how I got this one, and it is my husband's favorite dish to have at Thanksgiving dinner.

In a large mixing bowl, mix together the sour cream, cream cheese, granulated sugar, and vanilla until well blended. Fold in the grapes, then transfer the salad into a serving bowl. Sprinkle with the brown sugar, then arrange the pecan halves over the top. Cover and chill for at least 2 hours before serving.

COLESLAW

SERVES 6 TO 8

1 medium head green cabbage

2 medium carrots, shredded (about 1 cup)

Dressing

1 cup mayonnaise

1½ teaspoons yellow mustard

¼ cup sugar

¼ cup white vinegar

½ teaspoon coarsely ground black pepper

¼ teaspoon salt

Pinch of ground cumin

Pinch of chipotle powder

No side is as ubiquitous at a barbecue party as coleslaw. They just go together. Coleslaw in the South is kind of personal, and we get more comments about it in the restaurants than about any other item. People typically *love* the coleslaw their mama made, and they get pretty upset when they're served other versions. Well, this slaw is how my mother made it (with my own little twist), and that's the last thing I'll say about that!

Quarter the cabbage, slice out and discard the core, then make thin cuts down the face of each quarter. (You can give it a few more chops if you want smaller pieces.) Place the cabbage in a large bowl and toss with the carrots.

To make the dressing, place all the ingredients in a medium mixing bowl and stir well to mix.

Add 1 to 1½ cups of the dressing to the cabbage and toss to coat. The slaw should look moist but not too wet. (Coleslaw will weep after it sits.)

CABBAGE STEAKS WITH NDUJA AND SMOKED ONION SOUBISE

SERVES 4

Nduja and Smoked Onion Soubise

- 2 medium white or yellow onions, peeled
- 2 tablespoons salted butter
- 1½ cups heavy cream
- 3 ounces nduja
- Kosher salt and freshly ground black pepper

Cabbage Steaks

- 1 (3-pound) head green cabbage
- Olive oil
- 2 tablespoons SPG+ Seasoning (page 45)
- Drizzle of Herb Oil (page 42), for serving
- 2 teaspoons finely chopped fresh basil leaves, for garnish
- 2 teaspoons finely chopped fresh dill, for garnish

Cabbage steaks are one of my favorite things to grill in the summer. I love it when the edges get crispy and caramelized. In this recipe, I'm using nduja, a spicy spreadable salami from Calabria. The high fat content makes it spreadable, and it enhances a dish. I am taking a nontraditional approach by adding it to soubise, a French sauce made from onions, butter, and cream. Note: If you want this dish to scream summer, drizzle some salsa verde (page 62) over the steaks to kick it up a notch.

To make the soubise, preheat a grill to medium heat with a two-zone fire. Place the onions on a grill-safe tray and place on the cooler side of the grill. Smoke for 8 to 10 minutes to allow the onions to get some smoke flavor. Remove the onions from the grill and let cool slightly, then thinly slice.

Melt the butter in a large saucepan over medium heat. Add the onions and cook, stirring frequently, until the onions have softened and most of the liquid has evaporated, 5 to 10 minutes. Be careful not to let the onions brown.

Add the cream and nduja and stir to combine. Cook until bubbles start to form, about 2 minutes. Decrease the heat to low and let simmer for 4 to 5 minutes. Transfer the mixture to a blender or food processor and blend, starting at a low speed and gradually working up to high, until a sauce forms, 1 to 2 minutes.

Using a strainer, pour the sauce into the saucepan. Stir in salt and pepper to taste. Keep warm over very low heat until ready to serve.

To make the cabbage, cut the head of cabbage into four 1½-inch-thick steaks, leaving the core intact. Drizzle the olive oil on each steak and season with the seasoning. Place the cabbage on the grill and cook for 5 minutes on each side, or until charred on the outside and soft in the center.

To serve, spread the soubise on a platter, place the steaks over it, drizzle with Herb Oil (and salsa verde if you want), and garnish with basil and dill.

PIKLIZ (SPICY HAITIAN SLAW)

MAKES 1 PINT

- **Juice of one 1 lime**
- **1½ cups apple cider vinegar or white vinegar**
- **1 teaspoon kosher salt, divided**
- **3 to 4 sprigs thyme, stemmed and minced**
- **2 habaneros, seeded**
- **1½ cups shredded green cabbage**
- **1 red bell pepper, julienned**
- **1 large carrot, shredded (makes about ½ cup)**
- **1 medium sweet onion, julienned**
- **½ tablespoon black peppercorns**
- **4 cloves garlic, minced**

Pikliz is a common condiment in Haitian cuisine, but it needs more exposure than it has received. It has a bright, spicy flavor that I can't get enough of in dishes. It works well with many smoked or grilled items and brings a snappy complement to sandwiches, stews, and even a pot of beans. Scotch bonnets are the traditional chiles used but are rather hard to find in my neck of the woods, so I substitute orange habaneros. White vinegar is traditionally used, but I prefer apple cider vinegar. Vary the amount of habaneros to the level of spice you want. This will become your must-have accompaniment for hot dogs and hamburgers!

NOTE: Be sure to wear gloves when handling the habaneros.

Place the lime juice, vinegar, ½ teaspoon of the salt, thyme, and habaneros in a food processor or blender and process to create a brine.

Place the cabbage, bell pepper, carrots, onion, peppercorns, and garlic in a mixing bowl and toss to combine. Sprinkle with the remaining ½ teaspoon salt, put the mixture in a quart mason jar, and tamp down to fit. Pour in the brine, screw the lid on, and let the vegetables pickle in the fridge for 3 days, shaking occasionally. Store in the refrigerator for up to 1 month.

CRISPY SMOKY BEEF TALLOW-ROASTED POTATOES

SERVES 2 TO 4

- **2 quarts water**
- **½ teaspoon baking soda**
- **1 tablespoon plus 1 teaspoon kosher salt, divided**
- **2 pounds russet potatoes, peeled and cut into 1½-inch chunks**
- **3 tablespoons Smoky Beef Tallow (page 43)**
- **½ tablespoon Smoke-Roasted Garlic (page 46) or minced garlic**
- **½ teaspoon black pepper**
- **1 teaspoon minced chives, for serving**
- **1 teaspoon minced rosemary, for serving**

Once I figured out how to perfectly roast a potato, I felt unstoppable. These are crispy, creamy, and so satisfying. The smoky beef tallow adds a great depth of flavor.

Fill a large pot with the water, add the baking soda and 1 tablespoon of the salt, and bring to a boil. Add the potatoes and cook until a knife is easily inserted into the potatoes, about 10 minutes.

Heat the beef tallow in a microwave until it's hot but not bubbling.

Drain the potatoes and return them to the pot. Pour in the beef tallow, season with the garlic, the remaining 1 teaspoon of salt, and the pepper, and fold into the potatoes until they have a "roughed-up" appearance. (Do not break up the chunks.)

Preheat the oven to 425°F. Spread the potatoes on a sheet pan, roast for 25 minutes, and loosen any stuck potatoes. Roast for another 20 to 25 minutes, or until the potatoes are brown and crispy. Sprinkle with the chives and rosemary.

BAKED BEANS FROM SCRATCH

SERVES 4 TO 6

- 1 pound great Northern or navy beans, soaked overnight and drained
- 6 slices bacon
- 1 medium yellow onion, diced
- ½ green bell pepper, diced
- 1 tablespoon minced garlic
- 1½ teaspoon kosher salt
- 1 teaspoon black pepper
- 2 cups ketchup
- ¼ cup Melissa Cookston Woo Woo Sauce or Worcestershire sauce
- ⅓ cup maple syrup
- ½ cup water
- ¼ cup Tabasco Chipotle Pepper Sauce
- 1 tablespoon Classic BBQ Rub (page 38)

Baked beans are a classic BBQ side that pairs well with so many dishes. When I was a kid in the Mississippi Delta, my mom and I would drive all the way to Memphis some Saturdays just for our favorite baked beans (and maybe some shopping). I have since learned that it is so easy to make baked beans from scratch, and this recipe is now my new favorite.

Place the beans in a stockpot and add enough water to cover them plus about 1 inch above. Bring to a boil, then simmer for 1 hour, adding water as needed, then drain.

Line a plate with a paper towel. In a skillet on medium-high heat, cook the bacon until crisp. Transfer the bacon to the plate and let cool, then crumble. Leave half of the rendered fat in the pan and discard the rest.

Place the onion and bell pepper in the pan and cook for 3 to 4 minutes, until the vegetables are softened but not translucent. Add the garlic and cook for 1 minute, then remove from the heat.

Preheat the oven to 350°F. In a large baking dish, mix together the beans, onion mixture, and the remaining ingredients. Bake for 1½ hours, stirring occasionally, or until the beans are tender and the liquid has thickened around the beans.

RED BEANS AND RICE

SERVES 3 TO 4

- ½ tablespoon avocado oil
- 1 pound smoked sausage, cut into half-moons
- 1 green bell pepper, sliced
- 1 red bell pepper, sliced
- 1 medium yellow onion, sliced
- 1 medium rib celery, diced
- 2 tablespoons minced garlic
- 4 ounces tasso ham or regular ham (optional)
- 2 to 3 bay leaves
- 1 teaspoon kosher salt
- 1 teaspoon coarsely ground black pepper
- ½ tablespoon Cajun seasoning
- ½ teaspoon cayenne pepper (optional)
- 1 quart chicken stock
- 1 pound small red beans, soaked overnight, drained, and rinsed
- Cooked rice, for serving

Red beans and rice is a hearty Mississippi Delta and New Orleans dish. This recipe features tasso ham, which I love using. Tasso ham isn't really ham but cured pork shoulder heavily seasoned with Cajun spices and smoked. I keep some in the fridge or freezer, as I love using it in many recipes. If you use regular ham instead of tasso, adjust the Cajun seasoning to your liking.

Heat the avocado oil in a large stockpot over medium-high heat. Add the sausage and sear for 3 to 5 minutes, stirring occasionally. Remove the sausage from the pot. Add the bell peppers, onion, and celery to the pot, and cook until softened and fragrant, 5 to 7 minutes. Then add the garlic, tasso ham (if using), bay leaves, salt, pepper, seasoning, and cayenne pepper (if using). Cook for 2 minutes.

Add the chicken stock, sausage, and beans to the stockpot and bring to a boil. Decrease the heat to a simmer, cover, and cook for 2 to 3 hours, or until the beans are softened. (Add water if the stew gets too dry.) Taste and adjust the seasoning as needed, and serve with cooked rice.

BROTHY WHITE BEANS WITH PARMESAN TUILLES

SERVES 4 TO 6

1 pound dried white beans
12 cups water, divided
¼ cup olive oil
1 medium yellow onion, quartered
3 to 4 sprigs thyme
3 to 4 sprigs rosemary
3 bay leaves
4 large cloves garlic
1 1-inch knob ginger, peeled
1 teaspoon red pepper flakes
1 Parmesan rind
4 cups chicken or vegetable stock
Kosher salt and freshly ground black pepper

Parmesan Tuilles

½ cup grated Parmesan
1 tablespoon red pepper flakes
Calabrian chili oil, for serving

Nothing is more comforting during the winter than a pot of beans simmering on the stove. This recipe takes me back to my childhood. I always loved the days I spent with my grandparents, and on chilly winter days, my grandmother would never fail to have a pot of beans on the stove. Tracy never wanted to be called "Grandma" or "Granny," so we called her by her first name. She was an eccentric grandmother who had many talents as an artist, a gardener, and a cook. She was one of the funniest people I've ever known. This is my homage to her.

White beans are very versatile, and this recipe can be modified in any fashion you like. You can substitute many different beans: lima beans (butterbeans), cannellini beans, navy, or great Northern beans. For this recipe, great Northern beans are my favorite. I use a quick soak method here, but you may soak your beans overnight instead.

For a quick soak, place the beans in a large heavy-bottomed pot or Dutch oven, and add 8 cups of the water. Bring to a boil for 1 minute, then turn off stove and let sit for 1 hour.

(continued)

Drain and rinse the soaked beans. Return them to the pot and add the olive oil, onion, herbs, garlic, ginger, red pepper flakes, and Parmesan rind. Add the remaining 4 cups of water and the chicken stock. Cover the pot and let it come to a gentle simmer. Cook for 45 minutes, then check for doneness and season with salt and pepper to taste. Cook for another 15 to 45 minutes, or until the beans reach your desired consistency.

To make the tuilles, preheat the oven to 400°F and line a baking sheet with parchment paper. Combine the Parmesan and red pepper flakes in a bowl. Place a heaping spoonful of the mixture on the baking sheet and pat down lightly. Repeat with the remaining mixture, spacing the spoonfuls ½ inch apart. Bake for 3 to 5 minutes, or until the tuilles are golden and crisp. Let cool.

Once the beans are cooked through, scoop out the herb stems, ginger, bay leaves, and Parmesan rind and discard. Plate the beans, drizzle with the chili oil, and serve with the tuilles.

9

SWEET TREATS AND COCKTAILS

BLUEBERRY BUTTER PIE WITH BLUEBERRY SAUCE

SERVES 6 TO 8

Blueberry Sauce

Makes 1½ cups

- 2 cups blueberries
- 2 cups sugar
- 1½ cups water

Blueberry Butter Pie

- 1 cup fresh blueberries
- 1 (8-inch) deep-dish pie crust
- 4 tablespoons (½ stick) unsalted butter, softened
- ½ cup buttermilk
- 3 large eggs
- ½ teaspoon pure vanilla extract
- 2 cups sugar
- ½ cup all-purpose flour
- Pinch of salt

Pie is always a good thing, and when you have fresh blueberries, it can be a great thing. This is my husband's favorite pie. Even though this doesn't have a lot of butter (what's ¼ cup between friends?), the pie's texture and its light crust are so delicious and buttery that I just call it a butter pie. It's not overly sweet but just right. In this recipe I'm calling for a premade pie crust, but you are welcome to make your own, although that means you will be 20 to 30 minutes further away from having a slice. The sauce is optional, as the pie is good by itself.

To make the sauce, place all the ingredients in a small saucepan and bring to a boil over medium-high heat. Decrease the heat to medium and cook at a low boil, stirring occasionally, to reduce until syrupy and thick, about 1 hour. Turn off the heat and let cool before serving. Will keep in the fridge for 3 days (if it lasts that long!).

To make the pie, preheat the oven to 350°F. Place the blueberries on the crust.

Using a mixer, beat together the butter, buttermilk, eggs, and vanilla in a mixing bowl at low-medium speed until the butter is cut into small pieces, about 1 minute. In a separate bowl, whisk together the sugar, flour, and salt, then add to the butter mixture. Mix on medium speed for 30 seconds, until incorporated. Pour the mixture over the blueberries. Bake for 55 to 60 minutes, until set. Check on the pie after 40 minutes and cover lightly with aluminum foil if the crust is browning too much.

To serve, drizzle 1 tablespoon of warm sauce on each slice.

SMOKED BASQUE CHEESECAKE WITH STRAWBERRY COULIS

MAKES 1 (8-INCH) CAKE

Basque Cheesecake

3 (8-ounce) packages cream cheese

1 cup sugar

1¼ cups whipping cream

2 teaspoons vanilla bean paste or extract

2 teaspoons rum

¼ cup all-purpose flour

4 large eggs, lightly beaten

Strawberry Coulis

1 pound strawberries, hulled and finely diced

½ cup sugar

2 tablespoons fresh lemon juice

Strip of lemon peel

Basque cheesecakes are a specialty of the Basque region of northern Spain and are very different from the popular New York cheesecake. Less sweet and sporting a dark caramelized crust, Basque cheesecakes lend themselves well to being prepared on a grill as they do not require a water bath to cook. For baking on a grill, I prefer to use a ceramic kamado grill with heat deflectors. You can also use a pellet grill or set up a charcoal or gas grill with a two-zone fire. (The cheesecake will bake on the cooler side.)

To make the cheesecake, preheat a grill to medium-high heat (about 425°F ambient temperature) with a two-zone fire. Scrunch up a piece of parchment paper and press it into an 8-inch pan. (A springform pan is preferred but not necessary.)

Beat the cream cheese in a stand mixer fitted with the paddle attachment or with a hand mixer on medium speed for 2 to 3 minutes, until all the lumps have been blended out. Add the sugar and mix on low speed for 10 seconds. Mix in the cream, vanilla, rum, and flour and mix until lump-free. While the mixer is running on the lowest setting, very slowly pour in the eggs. Stop the mixer as soon as they are fully incorporated to avoid air bubbles in the batter.

(continued)

Pour the mixture into the prepared pan. Set on the cooler side of the grill and bake for 45 to 55 minutes, or until the cheesecake surface is a deep golden brown. Remove from the grill and cool in the pan at room temperature for 2 hours. (Note that the middle will sink.) Then refrigerate, uncovered, for 8 hours or overnight. The cheesecake is best eaten within a day at room temperature.

To make the coulis, place all the ingredients in a medium saucepan over medium heat. Let the mixture come to a simmer, stirring occasionally to dissolve the sugar. Simmer for 10 to 12 minutes, or until the strawberries are softened. Remove the lemon peel and then use an immersion blender to purée the mixture. (You can also blend the mixture in a blender.) Use as is or pass through a sieve to make it smoother. The coulis can be stored in the fridge for up to 2 weeks. To serve, set the cheesecake out to come up to room temperature. Drizzle the coulis on each cheesecake slice.

GRILLED BLACKBERRY UPSIDE-DOWN CAKE

SERVES 4

- ½ cup (1 stick) plus 2 tablespoons salted butter, divided
- ¼ cup light brown sugar
- 2 cups fresh blackberries
- 1¾ cups granulated sugar, divided
- 1½ cups cake flour
- 1 teaspoon baking powder
- ¼ teaspoon baking soda
- ½ teaspoon salt
- 2 eggs
- 1 teaspoon pure vanilla extract
- ¼ cup milk

My grilled blackberry upside-down cake recipe covers a lot of territory for me. I am a blackberry fan, and I love grills. Further, I am partial to cake!

Mid- to late June/early July is when blackberries are at their peak in my area. In my early years, I spent many summer days picking them. Forging through the brush to reach the berry patch, making noise to scare off snakes, and trying to avoid thorns and chiggers didn't seem to be a big deal when I was younger. However, now I prefer to simply visit a farmers' market and get them without all the work. Plus, I love supporting local farmers and people who are attached to the land, like the people I grew up with.

Baking on the grill tends to give your goods just that little hint of "extra" you didn't know you were missing. I usually don't use wood to smoke when baking, as a cake or bread can get overwhelmed with smoke flavor easily. When I bake on a grill, I usually use my ceramic grill with heat deflectors as they have the most even heat.

Upside-down cakes are a favorite of mine because they are easy to prepare, look pretty, and taste even better. When I'm doing something like this on my grill, I always break out my trusty cast-iron skillet. It works well to make the blackberry syrup in the skillet and then pour the cake batter into it. While a pineapple upside-down cake is the most ubiquitous of these cakes, one made with fresh blackberries will shine with the brilliant purple they bring during the summer.

Heat a cast-iron skillet over medium-high heat. Place 2 tablespoons of the butter and the brown sugar in the pan, and stir to make a caramel. Add the blackberries and ¾ cup of the granulated sugar and stir. Press the blackberries with a spatula to break them up and release their juices. (You don't want them to cook into a purée—just broken down a bit.) Depending on how juicy your blackberries are, cook for 3 to 4 minutes, until they reduce slightly and form a syrup. Remove from the heat.

In a bowl, whisk together the flour, baking powder, baking soda, and salt. Using a stand mixer fitted with a paddle attachment, on high speed, beat together the remaining ½ cup butter and 1 cup of granulated sugar until the butter is incorporated, 2 to 3 minutes. Then add the eggs and mix to incorporate.

With the mixer running at low speed, add the flour mixture, vanilla, and milk a little at a time until all are incorporated.

Prepare a grill to cook at 350°F. Pour the batter over the blackberry syrup in the skillet. Using a spatula, tease the batter to the edges. Place the skillet in the grill and cook for 25 to 30 minutes, or until a toothpick inserted in the middle comes out clean.

Remove the skillet from the grill. Run a knife lightly around the edges of the skillet to release the cake, and let it sit in the skillet for 10 minutes to tighten up. Position a plate over the skillet, flip the skillet over, and slowly raise it to release the cake. (If the cake doesn't release, put the skillet on a stovetop over low heat for 3 to 4 minutes, then try again.) The cake will keep on the counter for 2 to 3 days.

SWEET CORN PIE

MAKES 1 (9-INCH) PIE

Pie

- 3 fresh corn cobs
- 1⅓ cups 2% milk
- 4 large eggs
- 1½ teaspoons salt
- ¼ cup granulated sugar
- ½ cup light brown sugar
- 1½ teaspoons pure vanilla extract
- 1½ teaspoons apple pie spice

Sauce

- 3 tablespoons sweetened condensed milk
- 1 tablespoon milk
- Pinch of salt
- Pinch of apple pie spice (optional)

- Whipped cream, for garnish
- Mint leaves, for garnish

I grew up in the country, and corn was a staple in our garden and at our table. I've loved corn in all its forms—freshly cooked corn on the cob, creamed corn, maque choux, cornbread, grits, etc.—ever since. But I had never had a sweet corn pie until I visited Guatemala. It was so delicious that I knew I had to re-create it. After several attempts, I'm happy with this version, and I hope you will be, too. You can use any eggs, but farm or organic eggs will enhance the color of the pie.

To make the pie, preheat the oven to 400°F. Grease a 9-inch pie pan. Using a sharp knife, cut the kernels off each corn cob into a large plate with a lip, leaving just a bit attached to the cob. Use the back of the knife to scrape downward over each cob to help release any remaining corn milk. Measure out 2 cups of kernels/corn milk. Reserve any extra kernels for garnish.

Place the kernels in a blender and pulse a few times to shred them. If you like pulpy orange juice, do this only a couple of times for more texture; if you like smooth OJ, purée it.

Place the remaining pie ingredients in a large bowl and whisk thoroughly. Add the kernels/corn milk and whisk to incorporate. Pour the mixture into the pie pan.

Bake the pie for 10 minutes, then decrease the temperature to 350°F. Continue to bake until the middle is puffed up and the pie is set. Remove from the oven and let cool for at least 20 minutes.

To make the sauce, place the condensed milk, milk, salt, and apple pie spice, if using, in a small bowl and whisk to combine.

To serve, drizzle each pie slice with the sauce, and garnish with the remaining corn kernels, whipped cream, and a mint leaf.

FAT-WASHED MINT JULEP

SERVES 6 TO 8

Fat-Washed Bourbon

6 slices bacon

1 (750-ml) bottle bourbon

Simple Syrup

2 cups water

2 cups sugar

2 to 3 bunches fresh mint, stemmed and coarsely chopped

Crushed ice

Fresh mint leaves, for garnish

When you cook whole hogs, you tend to get to know the other whole-hog cooks. As the competitions run through the night, there's a good bit of wandering around, telling of tall tales, and expressing disdain for the judges. (As any competition cook will tell you, it's *always* the judge's fault when you don't win.) I have a good BBQ buddy named Jim who often had a whiskey drink in his hand. One morning at about 5:00 a.m., he was strolling around with a beer, something I had not seen him with before. I asked him what was up with drinking beer at 5:00 a.m., and he answered, "It keeps me off the whiskey." I still tell this story twenty years later and chuckle.

Mint juleps have been served in the millions just at the Kentucky Derby, and though they have their place as the traditional Kentucky Derby cocktail, I think we can take the julep to a whole 'nother level. This recipe features a method for "fat washing" the bourbon. (And don't try to sneak any whiskey into this recipe other than an official Kentucky bourbon.) Fat washing, or infusing liquors with extra flavor through bacon fat, beef tallow, or even butter, helps turn this classic cocktail into a memorable event. I use bacon grease for this recipe because everything is better with bacon!

(continued)

To make the bourbon, in a skillet over high heat, cook the bacon until the fat has rendered. Remove the bacon from the skillet and save for another use. (You can use some as a garnish and some for a snack.) Pour the bourbon in a quart mason jar (or any sealable container) and add the bacon fat. Let the mixture sit for a minimum of 4 hours, shaking occasionally. Place jar in the freezer for at least 4 hours. (Overnight is even better.) Strain the bourbon through a coffee filter, then pour it back into its original bottle. The bourbon will keep indefinitely.

To make the simple syrup, place the water and sugar in a saucepan. Simmer over medium-low heat, stirring until the sugar is fully dissolved and the syrup is clear, about 5 to 6 minutes. Turn off the burner, add the mint, and let steep for 20 to 25 minutes, stirring occasionally.

Remove the pan from the heat and let cool. Strain out the mint and pour the syrup into a glass container. It will keep in the fridge for about 1 week. (You can also use it in a nice glass of iced tea!)

To make the mint julep, fill a julep or highball glass with crushed ice. Add 2 ounces of the fat-washed bourbon and ½ ounce of the simple syrup. Garnish with mint leaves and a slice of bacon.

PISCO SOUR

SERVES 1

2 ounces Peruvian pisco
½ tablespoon egg white
2 ounces simple syrup (page 161)
1½ ounces Key lime juice
2 to 3 dashes bitters
Crushed ice
Sprinkle of Tajín

Pisco sour is the national drink of both Peru and Chile, as they both claim to be the originators of pisco. Pisco is a clear brandy, and this cocktail is the perfect pairing with Peruvian ceviche or anticuchos.

Add the pisco, egg white, syrup, Key lime juice, bitters, and crushed ice to a cocktail shaker. Shake well, about 1 minute. Using a cocktail strainer, strain the liquid into a chilled coupe glass. Sprinkle with Tajín.

SMOKED BERRY SANGRIA

SERVES 4

½ cup fresh blueberries

½ cup fresh strawberries, hulled and halved

½ cup fresh raspberries

¼ cup sugar

1 whole orange, cut into chunks

1 (750-ml) bottle red wine, such as Rioja (or Lambrusco if you want to add some pizzazz)

½ cup fresh orange juice

⅓ cup brandy

Ice

Berries, mint, and orange slices, for garnish

I love traveling to Spain, and I love red wine. I also love jamón de ibérico, which you can buy by the cone in the markets there. I'd happily have a cone of ham in one hand and a glass of sangria in the other. The smokiness of the berries in this recipe provides a nice mellow flavor and really enhances the drink.

Preheat a smoker to cook at 225°F. Place all the berries on a sheet pan and smoke for 10 to 15 minutes, just to let the berries get a subtle smoke flavor. Place the berries in a pitcher, add the sugar and orange, and muddle with a wooden spoon to break up the fruit and release the juices. Add the wine, orange juice, and brandy, and let steep in the fridge for 10 minutes or up to 3 hours. (The flavor will improve the longer you let it steep.)

Fill glasses with ice and garnish with berries, mint, and orange slices, then fill with the sangria.

GRILLED PEACH-THYME MARGARITA

SERVES 4 TO 6

- **1 tablespoon neutral oil**
- **5 ripe peaches (freestone preferred), halved**
- **1 teaspoon cayenne pepper**
- **20 ounces tequila (reposado preferred)**
- **10 ounces fresh lime juice, about 10 limes**
- **8 ounces Cointreau or Grand Marnier**
- **4 to 5 sprigs thyme, plus more for garnish**
- **6 ounces simple syrup (page 161)**
- **Agave syrup, for rim**
- **Melissa Cookston Chipotle Pecan Rub, salt, or Tajín, for rim**

Peach season is one of my favorite times of year, even though it coincides with late summer, which is unbearably hot in the South. Margaritas are a great way to cool off, and when made with a freestone peach and fresh thyme, it almost makes me forget about the 110°F heat index.

Preheat a grill to medium-high heat and oil the grates. Sprinkle the peaches with the cayenne pepper and place them cut side down on the grill. Cook until they have grill marks and are soft, 8 to 12 minutes (turn 90 degrees halfway through cooking time). Remove from the grill and let cool for 30 minutes.

Place the tequila, lime juice, Cointreau, thyme, and simple syrup in a blender. Add all but one of the peach halves and blend on high for about 2 minutes, or until smooth. Cut the remaining peach half into thin slices. Rim four margarita glasses with agave syrup and chipotle pecan rub, salt, or Tajín. Fill the glasses with ice and margarita, and garnish with a peach slice and thyme sprig.

ACKNOWLEDGMENTS

Writing a cookbook is not an easy task, and I couldn't do it without my family and team.

First, I would like to thank the guests and customers of Memphis Barbecue Company and The BBQ Allstars. We have some of the most loyal supporters I've ever known. If you're in the Memphis area, please stop by Memphis Barbecue Co. and give us a holler. We always have freshly cooked pork rinds, slow-smoked pulled pork, and flavorful ribs (ask for them muddy), along with a wide variety of other made-from-scratch dishes. If you're looking for anything BBQ or cooking-related, visit TheBBQAllstars.com and check out what we have. I curate everything in the store, and I love finding cool items that aren't in every big-box store.

I would like to thank Susie Fogelson, who has been instrumental in my completion of this book and has supported my thoughts and ideas. Susie is amazingly talented and a good person to boot.

My longtime friend Donnavun Thomas was so great at helping test dishes and was a fabulous sous-chef for the photo shoot.

I try to use Alex Flores whenever I need hair and makeup for a photo shoot. She's just plain awesome.

Thank you to photographer Ken Goodman for his amazing work on the book.

John Keegan was very helpful in testing recipes and assisting with the photo shoot.

My husband, Pete, has been my supporter, cooking partner, and travel companion for twenty-eight years and counting. Together we've tried to "taste the world." We still have a ways to go, but I'm ready to keep the adventures coming.

Most of all, I'd like to thank my daughter, Lauren, who is a talented cook herself and has been a massive help with this book.

melissa cookston
FLAVOR DUST
GARLIC PARMESAN
melissa cookston
FLAVOR DUST
MEMPHIS BBQ
PREMIUM SEASONINGS
NET WT. 6 OZ (170g)
MELISSA COOKSTON'S®
World Championship
BEEF
INJECTION AND SOAK
NET WT. 16 OZ (454g)
melissa cookston
FLAVOR DUST
LEMON PEPPER
PREMIUM SEASONINGS
melissa cookston
FLAVOR DUST
SPICY BUFFALO
PREMIUM SEASONINGS
melissa cookston
FLAVOR DUST
HONEY HABANERO
PREMIUM SEASONINGS
NET WT. 6 OZ (170g)
melissa cookston
Classic
PREMIUM SEASONINGS
melissa cookston
LUCKY 7
PREMIUM SEASONINGS
melissa cookston
COAL PLAY
PREMIUM SEASONINGS
melissa cookston
BOLD
PREMIUM SEASONINGS
melissa cookston
CHIPOTLE PECAN
PREMIUM SEASONINGS
melissa cookston
Honey Peach
PREMIUM SEASONINGS
MELISSA COOKSTON'S®
POULTRY
INJECTION & BRINE
NET WT. 16 OZ (454g)
melissa cookston
BOLD
COMPETITION STYLE • BARBECUE SAUCE
melissa cookston
SASSY
COMPETITION STYLE • BARBECUE SAUCE
melissa cookston
Melissa's
WOO WOO
Sauce
melissa cookston
ORANGE CHIPOTLE
GLAZE
CHERRY BOMB
HOT SAUCE
melissacookston.com
Candied Jalapeños
16 FL. OZ. (473mL)
MELISSA COOKSTON'S®
World Championship
PORK
INJECTION
NET WT. 16 OZ (454g)

METRIC CONVERSIONS AND EQUIVALENTS

METRIC CONVERSION FORMULAS

To Convert	Multiply
Ounces to grams	Ounces by 28.35
Pounds to kilograms	Pounds by 0.454
Teaspoons to milliliters	Teaspoons by 4.93
Tablespoons to milliliters	Tablespoons by 14.79
Fluid ounces to milliliters	Fluid ounces by 29.57
Cups to milliliters	Cups by 236.59
Cups to liters	Cups by 0.236
Pints to liters	Pints by 0.473
Quarts to liters	Quarts by 0.946
Gallons to liters	Gallons by 3.785
Inches to centimeters	Inches by 2.54

COMMON INGREDIENTS AND THEIR APPROXIMATE EQUIVALENTS

1 cup uncooked rice = 225 grams
1 cup all-purpose flour = 140 grams
1 stick butter (4 ounces · ½ cup · 8 tablespoons) = 110 grams
1 cup butter (8 ounces · 2 sticks · 16 tablespoons) = 220 grams
1 cup brown sugar, firmly packed = 225 grams
1 cup granulated sugar = 200 grams

APPROXIMATE METRIC EQUIVALENTS

Volume	
¼ teaspoon	1 milliliter
½ teaspoon	2.5 milliliters
¾ teaspoon	4 milliliters
1 teaspoon	5 milliliters
1¼ teaspoons	6 milliliters
1½ teaspoons	7.5 milliliters
1¾ teaspoons	8.5 milliliters
2 teaspoons	10 milliliters
1 tablespoon (½ fluid ounce)	15 milliliters
2 tablespoons (1 fluid ounce)	30 milliliters
¼ cup	60 milliliters
⅓ cup	80 milliliters
½ cup (4 fluid ounces)	120 milliliters
⅔ cup	160 milliliters
¾ cup	180 milliliters
1 cup (8 fluid ounces)	240 milliliters
1¼ cups	300 milliliters
1½ cups (12 fluid ounces)	360 milliliters
1⅔ cups	400 milliliters
2 cups (1 pint)	460 milliliters
3 cups	700 milliliters
4 cups (1 quart)	0.95 liter
1 quart plus ¼ cup	1 liter
4 quarts (1 gallon)	3.8 liters

Weight	
¼ ounce	7 grams
½ ounce	14 grams
¾ ounce	21 grams
1 ounce	28 grams
1¼ ounces	35 grams
1½ ounces	42.5 grams
1⅔ ounces	45 grams
2 ounces	57 grams
3 ounces	85 grams
4 ounces (¼ pound)	113 grams
5 ounces	142 grams
6 ounces	170 grams
7 ounces	198 grams
8 ounces (½ pound)	227 grams
16 ounces (1 pound)	454 grams
35.25 ounces (2.2 pounds)	1 kilogram

Length	
⅛ inch	3 millimeters
¼ inch	6 millimeters
½ inch	1.25 centimeters
1 inch	2.5 centimeters
2 inches	5 centimeters
2½ inches	6 centimeters
4 inches	10 centimeters
5 inches	13 centimeters
6 inches	15.25 centimeters
12 inches (1 foot)	30 centimeters

OVEN TEMPERATURES

To convert Fahrenheit to Celsius, subtract 32 from Fahrenheit, multiply the result by 5, then divide by 9.

Description	Fahrenheit	Celsius	British Gas Mark
Very cool	200°	95°	0
Very cool	225°	110°	¼
Very cool	250°	120°	½
Cool	275°	135°	1
Cool	300°	150°	2
Warm	325°	165°	3
Moderate	350°	175°	4
Moderately hot	375°	190°	5
Fairly hot	400°	200°	6
Hot	425°	220°	7
Very hot	450°	230°	8
Very hot	475°	245°	9

Information compiled from a variety of sources, including *Recipes into Type* by Joan Whitman and Dolores Simon (Newton, MA: Biscuit Books, 2000); *The New Food Lover's Companion* by Sharon Tyler Herbst (Hauppauge, NY: Barron's, 1995); and *Rosemary Brown's Big Kitchen Instruction Book* (Kansas City, MO: Andrews McMeel, 1998).

Saucy Adobo Wings with Herby Buttermilk Dressing (page 125)

INDEX

NOTE: Page numbers in *italics* indicate photo pages.

D

E

F

G

H

I

J

K

L

P

The authorised representative in the EEA is Simon and Schuster Netherlands BV, Herculesplein 96 3584 AA Utrecht, Netherlands. (info@simonandschuster.nl)

Andrews McMeel Publishing
a division of Andrews McMeel Universal
1130 Walnut Street, Kansas City, Missouri 64106

www.andrewsmcmeel.com

26 27 28 29 30 RLP 10 9 8 7 6 5 4 3 2 1

ISBN: 979-8-8816-0536-0

Library of Congress Control Number: 2025946775

Editor: Jean Z. Lucas
Art Director: Holly Swayne
Production Editor: Kayla Overbey
Production Manager: Jeff Preuss
Photographer: Ken Goodman

Photo Credits:
Angie Mosier: xi, 11, 25, 58, 60, 81, 82, 110, 128
Stephanie Mullens: xii, xviii, xxi, 3, 9
iStock photography: 12, 145